MW01075462

# GUINEA FOWL

### THE COMPLETE

### OWNERS GUIDE

**E**ssential facts tips and information about keeping Guinea Fowl. including; general care, feeding, health, housing, breeding, and much more.

### ADRIAN MARKS

Published by:

KARM Publishing

ISBN: 978-1-910915-08-0

Copyright © 2015; KARM Publishing

All rights reserved. No part of this publication may be reproduced, distributed, or transmitted in any form or by any means, including photocopying, recording, downloading from a website or other informational storage, retrieval systems, electronic or mechanical methods, without the prior written permission of the publisher/ author.

### Disclaimer and Legal Notice

The author has made every effort to ensure the accuracy of the information within this book was correct at time of publication. Whilst the author has tried to keep the information up-to-date and correct, there are no representations or warranties, express or implied, about the completeness, accuracy, reliability, suitability or availability with respect to the information, products, services, or related graphics contained in this publication for any purpose. The author does not assume and hereby disclaims any liability to any party for any loss, damage, or disruption caused by errors or omissions, whether such errors or omissions result from accident, negligence, or any other cause.

The methods described within this publication are the author's prior knowledge and/or personal thoughts and/or opinions and/or experience of the subject. They are not intended to be a definitive set of instructions for this subject. Other methods, instructions, opinions and materials may be available to accomplish the same end result. Again under no circumstance can the author/publisher accept legal responsibility or liability for any loss, damage to property and/or personal injury, arising from any error or omissions from the information contained in this publication or from failure of the reader to correctly and precisely follow any information contained within the publication.

### 3rd party sources/information:

The author/publisher has no control, and is therefore not responsible for the content, availability or nature of any third party websites or other publications listed herein. Access and use of information of third party websites or other publications, is at your own risk. Any website publication or the information listed within them should not be implied as an endorsement or recommendation by the author/publisher.

The information provided within this publication, is strictly for educational purposes and general informational purposes only. If you wish to apply ideas contained in this publication, you are taking full responsibility for your actions. Therefore, any use of this information is at your own risk.

### Additional Disclaimer and Legal Notice information:

You must not in any circumstances:

a) publish, republish, sell, license, sub-license, rent, transfer, broadcast, distribute or redistribute the publication or any part of the publication;

b) edit, modify, adapt or alter the publication or any part of the publication;

c) use of the publication or any part of the publication in any way that is unlawful or in breach of any person's legal rights under any applicable law, or in any way that is offensive, indecent, discriminatory or otherwise objectionable;

d) use of the publication or any part of the publication to compete with us, whether directly or indirectly; or

e) use the publication or any part of the publication for a commercial purpose

#### (1) No advice

The publication contains information about Guinea Fowl. The information is not advice, and should not be treated as such. You must not rely on the information in the publication as an alternative to (legal/medical/veterinary/ financial/accountancy or other relevant) advice from an appropriately qualified professional. If you have any specific questions about any (legal/medical /veterinary/ financial/accountancy or other relevant) matter you should consult an appropriately qualified professional.

#### (2) Limited Warranties

We do not warrant or represent that the use of the publication will lead to any particular outcome or result.

#### (3) Limitations and exclusions of liability

We will not be liable to you in respect of any business losses, including (without limitation) loss of or damage to profits, income, revenue, use, production, anticipated savings, business, contracts, commercial opportunities or goodwill.

We will not be liable to you in respect of any loss or corruption of any data, database, hardware or software. We will not be liable to you in respect of any special, indirect or consequential loss or damage.

#### (4) Trademarks

Registered and unregistered trademarks or service marks in the publication are the property of their respective owners. Unless stated otherwise, we do not endorse and are not affiliated with any of the holders of any such rights and as such we cannot grant any licence to exercise such rights.

#### (5) Digital rights management

You acknowledge that this publication is protected by digital rights management technology, and that we may use this technology to enforce the terms of this disclaimer.

## About the Author;

Adrian Marks has been involved with animals his whole life. He has reared and kept many breeds of poultry over the years, including varieties of Ducks, Geese, Pheasant, Chickens, Bantams and of course Guinea Fowl. Guinea Fowl in particular have always held a lasting interest to him, which largely inspired him to pay homage to this fascinating bird. He considers it an absolute privilege and labour of love to be involved in this publication.

## Acknowledgements

As for work put into the creation of this book I would like to thank my parents and family for their perpetual love and support. They have never discouraged my deep and lasting interest in all animals whether wildlife or domestic. I thank them with much gratitude for not only encouraging me, but indulging me from a young age when I have wanted to add to our ever increasing collection.

# TABLE OF CONTENTS

If you are reading this information as an experienced poultry keeper, then parts will already be familiar to you. Having said that, the information is intended for everyone and I am sure that even the experienced poultry person will find a lot of new facts and information.

It is not my intention to patronize the reader and to tell you how you should read a book. However, unless you are an experienced poultry person and are confident enough to skip certain sections, I would highly recommend that you thoroughly read all of the contents before you begin to implement any of the instructions. You may wish to take notes as you go or re-read the book a second time noting important steps to give yourself an action plan.

# CHAPTER ONE

# INTRODUCING THE GUINEA FOWL

This Chapter will give you an introduction to Guinea Fowl. You will find information relating to: What they are; The different breeds; What they are like; why keep them, and much more

## 1) About Guinea Fowl

### a) What are Guinea Fowl?

Guinea Fowl are related to the family known as *Galliformes,* which includes pheasants. Although similar to game birds such as pheasant and partridge, Guinea Fowl are commonly known as a type of poultry. The most common known poultry type is the domestic chicken. As well as being kept as pets, Guinea Fowl, not unlike chickens and other poultry, are raised for their meat and eggs.

Perhaps because of their relation to pheasant, Guinea Fowl are known as game birds. In fact they have often been referred to and used as an alternative to pheasant for either meat or game shooting. The dark, lean meat is certainly reminiscent of pheasant. They also have very similar flight patterns to game birds. For example, they take off with an explosive burst. Generally flying for short distances and otherwise preferring to walk or run.

Of the eight known species of Guinea Fowl, the most common in captivity are the *Common or Helmeted Guinea Fowl, Crested Guinea Fowl* and the V*ulturine Guinea Fowl.* The *Common Helmeted* as mentioned, are the birds most people think of when asked about Guinea Fowl. They are the bird of choice because they are hardy, and can live for as long as 20 years or more. They are also very easy to manage. They also produce eggs, rich and high in protein as well as an excellent meat yield.

The Crested and Vulturine Guinea Fowl, although not as readily available, are still purchased by enthusiasts. They are still rarer however and for this reason, even if you can find a pair, they are quite expensive. In general the Crested and Vulturine require more specialist husbandry. The environment or aviary should ideally resemble the conditions of their natural habitat. Vulturine in particular do not take kindly to the cold and therefore require heated housing for optimum results.

However unlike their precocious relative, the helmeted Guinea Fowl, they are more placid and therefore not as noisy. Certainly for the enthusiast, they would probably be well worth the effort.

### b) Why keep Guinea Fowl?

Guinea Fowl are a good addition to any poultry enthusiasts collection. They are what you might term, semi-domesticated poultry. No doubt because of their relation to pheasants and other game birds, they still retain a wild instinct.

Keeping Guinea Fowl is very similar to the keeping of other poultry such as chickens. However, do not make the mistake of thinking everything that applies to the upkeep of chickens, applies to Guinea Fowl. There are specifics that you need to be aware of which will be discussed throughout the book.

### c) Are Guinea Fowl easy to keep?

If you ask any poultry keeper, you will no doubt be told that the birds need a clean, draft free, disease free environment. So you provide suitable accommodation that is clean and has dry bedding. You feed them nutritious food, supplemented with vegetation necessary for digestion. You give them grit to aid digestion and for egg production. You provide clean fresh water on a daily basis. If you have the luxury of free range then so much the better. And you keep them safe from predators.

Those basic instructions, are more or less all you need to keep happy and healthy Guinea Fowl, or for that matter any poultry. In general they do not need any costly specialist equipment or accommodation and so are relatively easy to keep.

### d) What are common Guinea Fowl like?

As previously mentioned, Guinea Fowl, although now commonly domesticated, still retain much of their wild tendencies. In that respect, they are more inclined to roam and forage freely, and often away from the confines of your property.

If you were to describe the common Guinea Fowl, you would probably sum them up as appearing highly strung and intense. You could also add that they are, unpredictable, mistrustful, vibrant, comical, resilient, easy to rear and never dull.

Guinea Fowl are naturally very curious and suspicious of strangers and anything unusual or out of the ordinary. They are very vocal, and will naturally call out, quickly alerting their flock of any danger. with an alarming shriek, alerting all to the presence of a stranger. In this respect they make excellent watchdogs for any premises. They are therefore very much akin to guard dogs, who will bark as soon as they spot anything strange to them.

The common helmeted Guinea Fowl is very hardy, despite the warm climbs of Africa, where it originated. Although like any animal they will on occasion get sick, they are also relatively disease resistant.

They are known to be voracious foragers of weeds and weed seeds, insects from grasshoppers to aphids to mosquitoes etc. In fact if you have insect pests and weeds that invade your garden then there is a strong likelihood your Guinea Fowl will feed on them.

### e) What do Guinea Fowl look like?

The Common Helmeted Guinea Fowl are known for their distinctive horn like protrusion on the top of their head. Around the head and neck they are largely hairless. The effect of the naked head and neck on most Guinea Fowl is said to allow the birds to forage easily for prolonged periods of the day at high African temperatures. This is perhaps a similar phenomenon to bald people who seem to require extra headgear insulation in winter months. In such cases, as heat rises without the insulation, it would otherwise escape through the head more easily. In the case of the Guinea Fowl the relatively cooler blood that re-circulates is thought to keep the

*3*

body relatively cooler.

Unlike Crested and Vulturine, who are very distinctive and specifically marked, the common Guinea Fowl come in a variety of colors. Although the common/helmeted Guinea Fowl has many subspecies, the appearance is very similar. In particular the largely bald head and neck has an off white, bluish grey coloring with patches of red across the head and base of the beak. The strong curved beak is very similar. The main difference seems to be the size of wattles and in particular the size and curvature of the helmet. But despite those differences, the general appearance is very similar.

However, perhaps because of the inter breeding, this species of Guinea Fowl has many colors.

The most common coloring of the common Guinea Fowl appear to be white, grey, blue, brown and purple. Other possible colors include pearl, lavender, royal purple, coral blue, buff, porcelain, opaline, slate, brown, powder blue, chocolate, violet, bronze, sky blue, pewter and pied Although it is probably rare to find a pure blue or brown Guinea Fowl. What does seem common are the variations and mixes of those colors such as fawn, tan, chamois, violet and lavender. With the exception of coloring such as white, the feathers general have a speckled appearance.

Choosing the color

Incidentally, when you decide to purchase your Guinea Fowl, if you have the option of choosing the color, you may wish to consider picking a color that allow the birds to blend in to its surroundings. A white bird in the snow will be relatively hidden, but in most wild terrain will stand out like a sore thumb. A gray or brown Guinea Fowl however, will blend in very well and no doubt evade the site of a predator.

### f) What are Keets?

Whereas a baby chicken is known as a chick, the term '**keet**' is the unique name given to the young of the Guinea Fowl. Keets are so called up until they reach 12 weeks of age. From 12 weeks until they reach 52 weeks, they are known as '**young Guineas**' Beyond this the sexes are then differentiated when at less than a year old the female is known as a pullet, and the male, a cockerel. Over a year old the adult Guineas are known as the Guinea cock and Guinea hen, respectively.

## 2) REASONS FOR KEEPING GUINEA FOWL

In this section we will cover the key advantages of keeping Guinea Fowl.

## A) EARNING THEIR KEEP, CLEARING INSECTS AND WEEDS

Obviously most pets give their owners undoubted pleasure from merely their presence. But how many pets can you say save you money in pesticides and insecticides, to name a few uses, as well as the organic effect to the environment.

When given the opportunity to free range, they will forage and graze the land with military precision. Insects they will eat generally include; grasshoppers, beetles, aphids, moths etc. They can be destructive of plants, but usually they will tend to go for seedlings. So if you have plants, whether vegetable or otherwise, you should attempt to keep the birds off the bed, or protect the beds with netting or something similar. Guinea Fowl will earn their keep in this way, within the months of March to October (at least 7 months), clearing insects and weeds as previously mentioned. It is perhaps not fair to state that for the rest of the year, you will have to feed them. Winter feeding Guinea Fowl is surprisingly cheap, as you will discover later. Late fall (Autumn), through winter to Spring, will see the insects and vegetation dying off. The Guinea Fowl will therefore be unable to forage for vegetation and the protein the insects provide.

When insects start to emerge, usually starting March, your Guinea Fowl will avidly search for and consume as much as they can. In this respect this will constitute a large part of their diet. Ticks can be a problem worldwide and once people become aware of this advantage for keeping Guinea Fowl, a major advantage of the bird can be utilized. Most insects that we consider pests to crops etc, are food for the Guinea Fowl. Grasshoppers and locust have long been considered pests for crop growers. These prolific eaters of vegetation can wipe out acres of crops causing millions of dollars of damage. According to an article from the following source.

*http://newsdesk. org/2010/03/30/a-grasshopper-plague-is-at-hand-in-us/,*

in 2010 alone parts of the US including Idaho, Nebraska, Wyoming etc were facing a plague situation. This is very good news for Guinea Fowl, as they devour such high protein insects. Any insect that the Guinea Fowl are not particularly fond of food wise, they are likely to kill anyway.

## B) COMMERCIAL REASONS KEEPING

From a commercial point of view, Guinea Fowl are eaten as a meat product. As previously mentioned, the meat is very similar to game, and is often used as a substitute for more expensive game such as pheasant. There is certainly a demand for anyone interested, with several acres of land, to become a supplier to specialist restaurants.

Guinea Fowl feathers are often used as a decorative feature for arts and crafts.

## 3) GUINEA FOWL IN HISTORY

As you already know, Guinea Fowl are known as *Galliformes,* which is the order of birds that include, chickens, pheasant and turkey to name a few. They are known by their family name of *Numididae.* Guinea Fowl that we know today are said to originate from the African continent. However, there seems to be uncertainty as to whether they did actually originate from there. It is suggested that the first discoveries were in France and China when respectively a bone and fossil were found. These were said to be dated between 35 and 55 million years ago. In addition, approximately 2.5 million years ago fossilized remains were found in Czechoslovakia, that were a close match to the Guinea Fowl *Numida meleagris.* Around 2400 BC, the first documented reference of the Guinea Fowl appeared on murals found in ancient pyramids at Saqqara. Trading of exotic goods and riches spread not only throughout Africa, but many of the worlds great nations.

Again, there seems to be uncertainty as to whether the Greeks initiated the name *meleagris.* Greek legend has it that the sisters of Meleager, wept at his passing and literally died of grief. It is then thought that the Goddess Artemis in an act of empathy toward their plight, turned them into Guinea Fowl. The white spots common on the feathers of the Guinea Fowl are said to represent the tears of the grieving sisters. However it has been suggested that the name is merely an altered form of the word melanargis, which literally means black and white.

### a) MODERN HISTORY

At whatever point in time the birds were introduced into Europe, they are still known in Italy as the Pharaoh's birds. No doubt paying homage to the place they perceived as the origin. In Greece, they are referred to as the Numidian game bird. Again probably for the same reason, named after, Numidia which was an Ancient Libyan-Berber kingdom and now known to be the North African region of Algeria and western Tunisia. The birds were certainly populated on the Guinea Coast of East Africa when Portuguese traders were said to have rediscovered them around the 15th Century. It is therefore fair to assume, the name Guinea Fowl, that we commonly refer to, is as a direct result of the Portuguese rediscovery. It wasn't until the reign of Henry VIII, that Guinea Fowl were said to have populated England.

Guinea Fowl popularity increased throughout Europe, Americas' and the Far East during the 18th and 19th centuries. As birds raised for the table, Guinea Fowl were not surprisingly seen as an excellent alternative to seasonal game birds. In this respect the British Victorian era experienced a peak in their popularity. With the advent of the first world war, prices rose and Guinea Fowl along with geese and turkey were now a luxury item. Popularity in the USA peaked in the late 1930's when approximately 1 million birds were produced. By the mid 1950's however, this figure had significantly dropped to ¼ of a million.

## 4) ABOUT THE GUINEA FOWL FAMILY

As late as 1735 the classification *Numida meleagris* that we know today, was finally established.

Since the 18th century ornithologists have sought to classify birds into groups, species and subspecies. Sometimes confusion has arisen over the naming of a bird and several individual ornithologists have given a different name to the same bird. However despite this, there are considered to be 38 species and subspecies of Guinea Fowl. These 38 are grouped by four genera, and further divided into 7 species. What follows are the main classes, subclasses and families that the Guinea Fowl fits into. There are several subclasses and suborders that are missing from this list but these are the most recognized.

They are classed as *Aves*, which encompasses all birds

The next main lower class or order, is known as *Galliformes*. These are a large collection of ground feeding birds, such as turkey, pheasant, grouse and of course Guinea Fowl.

Within this collection we have the families of which there are four

1. *Numididae;* Guinea Fowl.

2. *Meleagrididae;* Turkey.

3. *Phasianidae;* Which is the largest of the four families and includes several subfamilies such as, pheasant, quail, pea-fowl, partridge etc.

4. *Tetraonidae;* Capercaillie, Ptarmigan, Grouse.

The Numididae; Guineafowl family is further classified as follows:
There are four genus

1. Acryllium

2. Agelastes

3. Numida

4. Guttera

The family, four genus, species and subspecies are probably better explained with the following diagrams:

*Acryllium;* more commonly known as the *Vulturine guineafow*l.

| NUMIDIDAE | FAMILY |
| ACRYLLIUM | GENUS |
| vulturinum | SPECIES |

Taking the information above we refer to the *Vulturine guineafowl* by its genus and then species, therefore *acryllium vulturinum.*

*Agelastes;* more commonly known as the *black guineafowl (agelastes niger)*and the *white breasted guineafowl (agelastes meleagrides)*

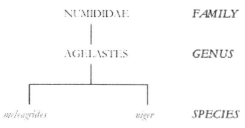

Things get a little more complicated when we introduce subspecies, but the principle is the same as follows:

Numida. More commonly known as common or helmeted guinea fowl (*numida meleagris*)

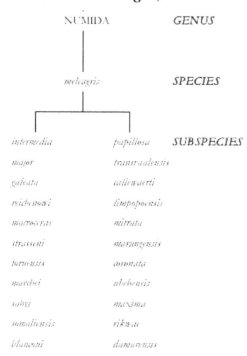

So taking the first *genus, species, subspecies,* we get *numida meleagris galeata.*

Last of all we have **Guttera;** More commonly known as the plumed or crested guinea fowl. Which again follows a similar pattern as above:

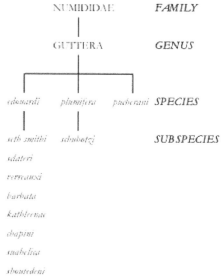

Again taking an example *genus, species, subspecies,* we get *guttera edouardi verreauxi,* and so on.

The following is a summary of the previous and of how Guinea Fowl have been scientifically classified. The most common species of Guinea Fowl will be covered in more detail shortly.

Biologists have sought to list and classify species into what is known as a 'Taxonomic order'. This simply gives the family tree as it were from the purist most primitive, through to the current blood line. So within each family or species, various subspecies have developed. This is a list of Guinea fowl species, presented in taxonomic order.

Guinea Fowl are classed as follows: (1) *order* (2) *family* (3) Species, *genera* or *genus*

5. They are known as belonging to the *order* of; *Galliformes*

6. The *family* name for Guinea Fowl is *Numididae*

7. The four species *genera* or *genus* are;

8. Numida

9. Guttera Agelastes

10. Acryllium

*Numida* are the most common and widely spread worldwide. These are the Guinea Fowl you are probably most familiar with as follows:

*1) Genus Numida include:*

Helmeted Guinea fowl, *Numida meleagris*

*2) Genus Guttera include:*

a) The Kenya Crested Guinea fowl, *Guttera (pucherani) pucherani*

b) The Crested Guinea Fowl, *Guttera (pucherani) edouardi*

c) The Plumed Guinea Fowl, *Guttera plumifera*

*3) Genus Agelastes include:*

a) White-breasted Guinea fowl, *Agelastes meleagrides*

b) Black Guinea fowl, *Agelastes niger*

*4) Genus Acryillium:*

Vulturine Guinea fowl, *Acryllium vulturinum*

The seven species above have become further subdivided into subspecies through inter breeding. It can be confusing when you realize that the helmeted Guinea fowl, *Numida meleagris*, has more than 20 sub species.

## 5) VULTURINE GUINEA FOWL

The Vulturine Guinea fowl *(acryllium vulturinum)* in its wild habitat, is known throughout Kenya, East Ethiopia, Somalia, as well as parts of Tanzania and Uganda.

They are commonly found in hot desert areas, scrub, wooded and grassland areas. Often seen in flocks of 20 to 70 or more birds. They are arguably the most spectacular of the Guinea Fowl and perhaps unsurprisingly labeled Royal. They are the largest of the Guinea Fowl with a length measuring anywhere from 23.5 inch to 27.5 inch approx, (60 to 70 cm). Their wing span is up to 10.5 feet (3.2 meters). They have coloring that is a striking mix of cobalt blue, black, white and grey. They also have the distinctive Guinea Fowl white spots covering most of their rear body. White stripes adorn the front of the bird from its neck to the breast and top of its wings. The head of the Vulturine, is probably more akin to a vulture, which the name undoubtedly derives. There is a single coloring of dark brown which appears as a tuft on the back of the birds head. As with all other Guinea Fowl the head and neck is largely bald.

A common characteristic of the Guinea Fowl species, is that the sexes are largely indistinguishable. The male Vulturine however, is slightly larger and should have at least one spur. They lay approximately 12 to 15 light brown/dark cream colored eggs that are around 2 inch (5 cm approx) long. They have an incubation period of approximately 24 days. In the same way as other Guinea Fowl, they will prefer to move by walking or running, rather than flying. However unlike the common helmeted Guinea Fowl, the Vulturine can abstain from water for a long time. In this respect they are extremely efficient in hot desert environments. They have a particularly voracious appetite for insects, and will forage for vegetation early in the day. They most likely obtain a great deal of moisture via these food stuffs. They are also said to be quieter, less vocal than the helmeted Guinea Fowl.

They are not as hardy as the helmeted Guinea Fowl, but are said to be easier to keep than certain exotic pheasant breeds. They can be adversely affected by extreme cold and damp weather. Under such conditions unless the building is well insulated, the birds need to be kept in a heated enclosure. However, it is suggested that a temperature above the early minuses, 28.4° F to 23° F (-2 to -5° C), should be bearable for them. Anything below that, would certainly need extra heating. The temperature within the house should be monitored in any case. Proper insulation and double glazed windows would be very beneficial in any case. With cold temperatures, the floor also needs insulating via either a thick litter of shavings or straw. It can be very uncomfortable for the birds to walk on any compacted flooring or concrete. They are also very good additions to a mixed poultry house, they are generally docile, unlike their more aggressive relations the helmeted. As the birds are rarer and therefore more expensive than the more common Guinea Fowl, many keepers do not take chances with incubation. The eggs are usually incubated artificially or using a broody hen. The Vulturine diet, as well as the aforementioned insects and vegetation can include,

Fruit, corn and other grains, minced meat is also a welcome dietary supplement for these birds.

## 6) THE BLACK GUINEA FOWL

The black Guinea fowl (*agelastes niger*), one of the two birds of the *agelastes* genus, again is so called because of its largely black covering. The bird is largely found in rain forest areas of Gabon, Cameroon, Congo and Zaire. They are therefore found roaming forest floors in small flocks of up to 25. This bird is unusual among Guinea Fowl as it is not a sought after bird for its flesh. The meat is not palatable and therefore not popular among the natives as a bird to be hunted. It is a relatively small bird with a length up to 45 cm (17 ¾ inches approx), and a wing span of 22 cm (8 ¾ inch approx). The bird most certainly resembles a Guinea Fowl, but is perhaps the most unremarkable of the family. As mentioned it is largely black and the bare head and neck is a bright pink red.

Again both sexes are alike with the exception that the male will have spurs, but to complicate matters, the female can also exhibit the occasional spur. These birds are also quiet with a softly repetitive call. As you may expect their diet consists of forest insects, vegetation and frogs. The eggs are usually a light brown color, around 4 cm (1½ inches approx) in length.

Although these birds have been kept in captivity, they do require a specialist environment resembling their natural habitat. For this reason they are probably not seen as a very viable option compared to say the Vulturine.

## 7) WHITE BREASTED GUINEA FOWL

The White Breasted Guinea Fowl (*agelastes meleagrides)*, the other bird included in the *agelastes* genus, is native to parts of Ghana, Liberia and the Ivory Coast. Although not on the verge of extinction, they are considered to be a vulnerable species under threat. Like the Black Guinea Fowl, they are to be found in tropical forests. They prefer well covered areas and are therefore not commonly spotted. When they have been encountered, they have usually been seen in pairs or small groups. They are up to 50 cm (19 ¾ inch approx) in length with a wing length up to 23 cm (9 inch approx). They are similar in appearance to the Black Guinea Fowl. They have a largely mono-colored dark brown/black covering. Again the head and neck are bare with the skin pink/red. As the name suggests, the breast covering is white.

The eggs are a pale rust brown of approximately 4.5 cm (1 ¾ inch) in length. Once again the sexes are alike with the male distinguishable by its spurs.

Their natural diets consists of forest seeds, leaves, insects etc. They have a low call, but they can make quite a loud melodious call on occasion. The birds have been successfully kept in captivity and similarly to the Black Guinea Fowl., they require a similar tropical environment.

Because of their status as under threat, there are many active conservation efforts at the moment, particularly in protected areas of Sierra Leone.

## 8) CRESTED/PLUMED GUINEA FOWL

The *guttera* genus, is commonly known as the **Crested Guinea Fowl**, or P**lumed Guinea Fowl**, depending on the species and subspecies.

So if you check back to the family tree for *guttera*, you will see that *guttera plumifera* is commonly known as the P**lumed Guinea Fowl.** Incidentally, if you check back to the family tree again you will notice there is 1 species and 1 subspecies. *Guttera pucherani*, of which there is 1 species known as the **Kenya Crested Guinea Fowl,** and no subspecies. However, *guttera edouardi*, and its many sub-species is also generally referred to as a **Crested Guinea Fowl**.

Whatever the specific nomenclature, the Plumed or Crested share one basic characteristic, that of a tuft of hair on the crown of the head.

Without going into the specifics of each species or subspecies, the *guttera* genus, whether *plumifera, pucherani* or *edouardi*, share similar characteristics as follows:

The *guttera* genus, can be found in tropical forested regions of East, West, Central and South Africa. They prefer the hidden area and are therefore rarely seen in the open.

The crest that is typical of this genus, varies in size and shape, depending on the subspecies. The color of the head and neck, which similar to other Guinea Fowl is mostly bare skin, also varies. Their stance is more upright, than the common Guinea Fowl. They have three calls, one of which resembles the relentless alarm call, typical of the common Guinea Fowl.

They feed on insects, seeds, forest vegetation, and are also known to feed on snails and spiders among others.

Once again they lay eggs on the ground in a secluded area. The eggs can measure up to 5 cm (2 inch approx) and be colored anything from whitish to light brown. They have an incubation period between 23 and 25 days.

Although this breed has been successfully kept and bred in captivity, they still require an environment similar to their native tropical rain forests.

This is a general overview of the *guttera* genus. Should you wish to know more specific information about the different species or subspecies, please refer back to the family tree. A quick search on the Internet will reveal additional information.

## 9) COMMON/HELMETED GUINEA FOWL

*Numida meleagris,* with over twenty subspecies, is the most prolific and commonly known of the Guinea Fowl species.

Among the subspecies it is commonly referred to as either the '**common or helmeted**'. However, depending on the subspecies other names include, grey

sion on the top of its head, hence the name helmeted. Between subspecies you will notice the length, shape and curvature vary. So if you come across a common/helmeted variety that has an unusually large, small or curved bony crown, then this may well be one of the may subspecies. The size and shape of the wattles, hanging from the base of the beak can also vary. However it is generally assumed that the size of wattles of specific species/subspecies, will only differ significantly between the male and the female. The male helmeted Guinea Fowl usually has larger and thicker wattles than the female. They will also vary in size and weight, again depending on species or subspecies.

Coloring also varies considerably throughout the species and subspecies. They are commonly light or dark grey with white speckles, but can be completely white, pearly white, white breasted, splashes of brown, etc. The bald head and neck area can be white, bluish white, cobalt blue, etc. Generally the wattles and top of the head are of a red/orange color.

They are not as particular or picky as some of their relations and will eat most foods if they have no choice. However, like all Guinea Fowl they will prefer insects, grains and vegetation.

Perhaps because of their distrustful and vigilant nature, these birds in the wild are highly successful against predators.

They are known to lay a clutch of anywhere between less than 10 and more than 20. Like the other genus and species, these Guinea Fowl, will lay eggs in a hollow in the ground, and equally prefer a hidden location. Several hens will share a nest and they are known to

breasted, Uganda Bristol nosed, Pencilled Guinea Fowl, crowned Guinea Fowl among others.

But, it is the helmeted that is the most popular of the species. It is generally populated over the far reaches of the whole of Africa, although the subspecies tend to be specifically located, and not so widely spread. They can therefore be found in mountainous regions of Morroco, desert regions of the Sahara and Arabia. They can also be found around damp saline coastal areas. They mostly prefer to roost in tall trees, so those areas will be commonly populated. Unlike the Vulturine, they cannot go without water for long, and will therefore be in close proximity to a watering hole or river. They are naturally voracious foragers and will walk for miles each day. This genus is unlike the other more private Guinea Fowl genus in its precocious, gregarious tendencies. In the mid twentieth century flocks of thousands of Guinea Fowl could be seen.

*Numida meleagris,* is most recognizable by its distinctive horn like protru-

take turns keeping guard. The hens even cover the nest with whatever is available, when she leaves. This is thought to not only camouflage the nest, but to retain moisture in the eggs. The egg coloration is a variation from whitish to light brown, and are up to 5.5 cm (2 ¼ inch approx) in length. Incubation is the same as for the domesticated birds i.e. between 26 and 28 days. Newly hatched keets have to grow up fast. Although the hen isolates herself from the flock during incubation, she soon rejoins when the keets are a couple of days old.

The coloring of the keets is similar to the pheasant chick. The light brown with black striping is typical, but some resemble the light grey of the adult. They retain the feathered covering, but lose this covering of the head and neck, towards adult hood.

The common helmeted Guinea Fowl is more hardy than the other genus of the family, but still need protection against extreme cold and damp weather.

Wing span is around 75 cm (29 ½ inch approx)and their length is approximately 55 cm (21 inch approx). But in some cases they can be slightly longer than this, occasionally over 60 cm (23 ½ inch approx).

The common Guinea Fowl is similar in size to a chicken, but is considered to be more finely boned. The average weight from adolescent bird to adult can range between 1 kg (2.2 pound approx) to 1.8 kg (4 pound) give or take, and depending on the sex. The male being slightly heavier than the female. They are said to have an average body temperature of approximately 107.6° F (42° C)

They will take flight if necessary but prefer moving over ground on foot. This may be to conserve valuable energy used up during flight, or perhaps they feel safer and more able on the ground.

The other subspecies noted in the family tree list have slight variations, but the species in general share many similarities. For anyone interested in researching the finer details of the subspecies please do check the family tree list. Once again, you should be able to locate this information on one of the many excellent resources on the Internet.

# Chapter Two

# What You Should Know Before Committing

**B**efore we get into the detail of keeping Guinea Fowl, you need to ask yourself some important questions. The following will provide an overview of what you will need in order to successfully keep Guinea Fowl. Included are the costs associated, as well as the pros and cons.

## 1) PRELIMINARY CONSID-ERATIONS

### A) DO YOU HAVE SUFFICIENT SPACE?

You may have your heart set on a flock of Guinea Fowl roaming your property, but unless you have sufficient space, you may well have to settle for a couple. In the majority of cases most backyard poultry keepers will probably have enough space for 6 to 10 birds. If you keep chickens you will no doubt keep them locked up over night and during the day, allow them to free range and roam about your garden. With Guinea Fowl this is not always possible nor advisable. Most poultry keepers with experience of Guinea Fowl will advise you to have a pen large enough for them to roam about free range. With chickens you can clip their wings and generally expect them to stay within your garden. Guinea Fowl on the other hand are instinctively programmed to roam and wander. If the perimeter of your property has a high fence, then providing you clip the birds wings they are unlikely to be able to escape. Without such a fence and wing clipping, the chances are, the birds will disappear and you may never see them again. So again, what you need to consider is, do you have sufficient space to either erect a high fence or have a large pen, that keeps the birds enclosed? We will cover the specifics of this throughout the book and advise you of what you will need, as we go. You will not need a football pitch or tennis court sized garden, but it is just worth baring in mind you will need a good sized area.

### B) DO YOU NEED A PERMIT?

This will vary depending on the area you live, so you should check with your local council, that you are actually permitted to keep Guinea Fowl for your area. If you live in a country, rural or perhaps semi rural area, you should have no problems, but again please do check this. If on the other hand you live in a built up urban area, there may already be certain restrictions that apply to keeping animals and in particular Guinea Fowl.

### C) WILL THE NEIGHBORS APPROVE?

If there are no local authority restrictions, you may still receive objections from neighbors. Many back yard enthusiasts who keep chickens have been known to have the odd neighborly objection to cockerels crowing at the crack of dawn. Guinea Fowl are known for the persistent noise levels they can emit anytime from dawn to dusk. So again it may be worth checking with local neighbors to alert them of your intentions. Once you educate them on the notable benefits such as pest and weed control, they may welcome your new additions.

## D) HOW MANY GUINEA FOWL?

This again has a lot to do with the available area you have, but please consider the following information also. There is much debate as to what constitutes an ideal or minimum number of Guinea Fowl. If you wonder what an ideal number is, then consider the numbers that make up the flocks seen in the African wilds. This number can range into hundreds for one flock. Obviously it is not expected that the average keeper can accommodate that many, or even want to. However, you are advised, and most keepers would advise taking no less than 8 or 10 birds.

### e) Minimum purchases. What choices do you have?

However, you may find that certain hatcheries have a minimum purchase requirement. There is also the unfortunate drawback with mail order, that despite their best efforts to carefully pack and ship these as fast as possible, some keets may turn up dead for a variety of reasons. You should also bear in mind that mortality at any stage of their development is a possibility. For this reason, once you decide to purchase a specific number, if you are restricted by a minimum order, bear in mind the fact some may die at some point anyway. So taking more birds will save you the trouble of sending for more later. If you manage to raise them all anyway then there is always the possibility that a friend or relative will be happy to take the surplus.

You will also find that whichever supplier you choose, you should get a choice of color, if you have a particular preference.

### f) Advantages of flock size

What you need to be aware of as a prospective keeper, is that Guinea Fowl prefer to be part of a big flock, as they are social and gregarious creatures.

It is not fair to generalize on this, but experienced keepers usually note that the bigger the flock, the more harmonious the birds seem to be. Whether this is because the birds feel safer and therefore happier in numbers is not certain. But it has to be said that fights and squabbles can be quite frequent were the numbers are less. That is not to say you should never consider less than 8 for example. You may only wish to keep a pair, i.e. a hen and cock, and it is unlikely they will fight. However many more problems get reported with smaller flocks experiencing aggressive, violent behavior leading to fights and injuries. Not to mention, more frequent disturbed birds with regular noise outbreaks. This is merely advice, and the choice is of course one you need to make for yourself, depending on your circumstances.

## 2) THE COST OF KEEPING GUINEA FOWL

The cost of feeding up to a dozen or more Guinea Fowl would probably work out a lot less than a family pet dog, for example.

The following will offer some basic guidelines as to prices you may pay. A lot depends on the size of coop and run you will need, and that obviously depends on the number of birds you want. We will look into specifics of construction later. For now you will be presented with the basics you will need as well as possible costs.

Apart from the cost of birds, your main set up costs will include.

### a) Coop/Hen House

This can be anything from a converted shed to a bespoke design. You are also advised to construct a wire enclosure/run. This allows the birds to free range, safe from predators and ensuring they don't escape. This is very similar to an aviary that has a house and a wire framed run to give the birds fresh air and space to stretch their legs.

### b) Housing Costs:

For a DIY coop, you may decide to convert a shed, relatively cheaply. A purpose built coop depending on the design and size in terms of how many birds it houses could be from $200 to $2,000 (£130 to £1300). A shed that you purchase could easily be in the same price range, but you will probably get a bigger size for your money. The resources section is a useful start for coops to purchase, or give you a few ideas for your own DIY project.

### c) Outside run:

If you build your own, you can no doubt source timber, perhaps reclaimed, fairly cheap. The total costs can vary but $500 (£325) will probably be the most you will pay for timber and wire roll chicken wire or sheets, to cover the frame.

If you have the funds available you may find that a custom built place is preferable. You would need to shop around or get a number of quotes, but do not be surprised if you do not have much change out of $1000 (£650 approx), for a basic unit. This can of course escalate into thousands depending on size and features.

### d) Feeders and drinkers

This again depends on the size of your set up and the number of birds you will keep. I would suggest, one feeder and two drinkers should be sufficient for 10 to 30 birds. Two 3.5 gallon plastic drinkers will probably cost you $40 (£26). A good quality galvanized 12lb capacity hanging feed hopper will cost about $17 (£11)

### e) Cost of each bird.

Costs will vary from breeder to breeder, but expect to pay around $5 (£3.25) to $20 (£13) each for helmeted keets.

### f) Food costs:

This will depend on the time of year. If the birds are free range, they will pick up a lot of protein food via insects and growing vegetation. You will probably supplement this with commercial feed

A number of breeders I know agree that a good rule of thumb is that if the birds are free ranging they will eat about 1lb to 1.5lb of feed per week per bird. In winter this could easily double to 2 – 3lb per bird per week of feed.

If free ranging is not an option, again this will be around 3lb of feed per bird per week.

If you buy your feed in 50lb bags, as an average let us say a bag of Purina Layena Pellets Premium Poultry Feed, 50 lb. would cost you $15 (£9.85) from for example the following supplier

*http://www.tractorsupply.com*
*http://www.tractorsupply.com/tsc/*
*catalog/chicken/chicken-feed-treats#f*
*acet:&productBeginIndex:20&orde*
*rBy:&pageView:grid&minPrice:&*
*maxPrice:&pageSize:20&*

Each bird could cost at 1lb per week, $0.30 (£0.20) per bird. Or at 3lb per week, $0.90 (£0.60) per bird.

My advice is buy a brand name to start with and then shop around your local area. You may find a feed mill that mixes their own and sells a lot cheaper than some of the brand names for the same quality.

Alfalfa is often used as vital vegetation feed particularly during winter. A bale of alfalfa will weigh about 100 pounds (45 kg approx). 30 birds can get through about 8 or these bales, which should last 4 or 5 months during winter.

For example an approximate bale weight of 100lb will cost about $20 (£13). Some suppliers sell by the tonne at around $200

1 tonne is about 2200lb, so you would get 22 bales, which at $20 (£13) would cost you $440 (£290). So it is well worth considering if you can buy in bulk.

So for example, if we say 30 birds get through 8 bales, so 100 x 8 = 800lb during a 4 or 5 month winter cold spell. Some areas will only have a 3 or 4 month

winter spell, before things start growing again.

Therefore one bird would use approximately 800 divided by 30 = 27lb. So one bird would use about 27lb of alfalfa during winter, which works out at less than $5 (£3.25) per bird. About $1 (£0.65) per month.

### g) Other costs:

You may from time to time need medications or the services of a Veterinarian. Again, it is difficult to generalize as to what this may be, but I should imagine you could set a budget of around $200 (£130) for the year.

### h) Grit

Grit is another essential for Guinea Fowl and again is very cheap. They will need a constant supply of this, so a dispenser should be made available. How much they consume depends on whether they free range and therefore how much gravel and other stone granules they will pick up free ranging. However, they will not consume a great deal. So depending on how many birds you have, a 50lb bag costing about $10 (£6.50) should easily keep you going a few months or more.

*http://www.tractorsupply.com/*
*tsc/product/manna-pro-oyster-shell-*
*50-lb?cm_vc=IOPDP1*

### i) Sawdust and Straw

Straw, you would mainly need for nesting boxes and sawdust would be best used as loose litter on the floor of the coop. You may well have a local supplier who can sell cheap straw bales. I have seen many advertised on ebay for around $2.20 (£1.50) per bale. Sawdust may be available free if you have a local saw mill/wood manufacturer. Again ebay is a good place to look if you have someone selling collection supplies only near you. 15kg bags would only cost about $1.50 (£1). If all else fails your local feed or pet supplier will no doubt stock these items

As you can see, other than the initial purchase costs, these ongoing costs are very minimal.

## 3) ADVANTAGES OF KEEPING GUINEA FOWL

We have already looked at some positive and negative characteristics of Guinea Fowl, but here we will touch on a few not already mentioned.

Guinea Fowl have many positive attributes, not to mention a hardy disposition and excellent foragers of insect pests and weeds. They are relatively self sufficient, low maintenance and therefore require very little specialist care and attention.

### a) Excellent Watchdogs

Quite often your Guinea Fowl will alert you to intruders before most guard dogs are aware. They have a natural suspicion of anything unusual and will freely vocalize this. The downside to this is the persistent noise they can make. We will talk more about possible solutions to problems of noise. But for the time being although they do make excellent watchdogs, they can also be noisy at times.

### b) Free fertilizer

On a free range setting guinea droppings could add valuable free fertilizer. Obviously it is not necessary to clean this up after them, however, if there are too many birds per acre, it could produce too much nitrogen. The effects of this is that the ground turns sour and makes new vegetation growth difficult. The Guinea Fowl droppings are generally dry, but on occasion do make a runny mess

### c) Hardiness

Although native to the hot climate of Africa, they are tolerant of the colder parts of the Northern Hemisphere. So providing they had sufficient insulated shelter, they could withstand colder parts of Europe, Scandinavia and North America.

### d) Earning their keep

Your guinea hens will lay eggs that you can either eat or sell, or perhaps breed your own keets. If you breed them you can sell surplus keets, whether day old or so many weeks old, or even adult birds. If you manage Guinea Fowl correctly and do not over feed with supplementary food, they will consume a lot of the insect pests and weeds that may otherwise plague your property. Guinea Fowl usually do not lay eggs all year round. However, during their laying season it is not unusual for them to lay one egg per day. Incidentally you should always aim to collect the eggs each day, particularly if you intend to use them for consumption.

In a nutshell they have many uses including; a source of protein rich eggs, excellent watch dogs, pest and weed controllers, highly amusing and entertaining.

## 4) DISADVANTAGES OF KEEPING GUINEA FOWL

### a) Guinea Fowl can be destructive.

If you keep your Guinea Fowl confined in a large open enclosure, then the following is unlikely to apply. If however your Guinea Fowl are entirely free range, then the following could apply.

They have very strong beaks that can peck and tear anything they choose to. So have a look around your property and see if you have any fabric, wooden or plastic materials that they could target to destroy. Also be aware they can also be quite destructive of plants

Lawns, flower and vegetable beds

They are not scratchers of earth in the same way that chickens are, but they do scratch whilst foraging. Flower or vegetable beds and lawns etc may well be attractive places to scratch. They could also choose to scratch the earth if they decide to take a dust bath in a flower bed or some other inappropriate place.

### b) Creating a mess; perching on roof tops etc

Do not expect them to be discriminating of where they perch. You can find them on roof tops, lean-to's in fact anywhere that suggest a perch for them. This in itself is not harmful, but whilst perching they can be readily dropping feces. So you may find that driveways, vehicles, path ways etc all have the potential to become messy if left.

While the birds are busy doing this on your property this may be fine for you. However, this could all be repeated once they leave your boundary and enter a neighbors property.

### c) Noise

As previously mentioned, an unfortunate drawback is the noise they can make. There is no getting away from it, Guinea Fowl can be loud and sometimes persistent. If your nearest neighbor was a mile away, they may not notice if your Guinea Fowl make a racket. But a neighbor 100 yards (91.4 meters) away, most certainly would. If they were not disturbed by the sound, any one closer than that most likely will be. To say the least, you certainly need tolerant, understanding neighbors, if you are in any kind of built up area.

# CHAPTER THREE

# BUYING GUINEA FOWL

This chapter will cover your options for purchasing guinea fowl. We will look at your three main options; buying adult birds, keets or hatching eggs. You will also be presented with a number of suppliers both in the U.S.A and the U.K.

# 1) BUYING ADULT BIRDS

## A) PROBLEMS WITH BUYING ADULT BIRDS

Given the choice you would not be advised to purchase mature Guinea Fowl. You may be lucky and find that mature birds that you purchase have been hand reared from young and are very tame. They will still doubtless be naturally suspicious and wary of your new surroundings. However, they should not be as problematic as a bird that has been reared semi wild, with little or no human contact.

Adult birds that you acquire can also disappear if you have the birds running free range. If the birds have been trained to come back to their previous hen house at night, after foraging then it is only natural that they will attempt to do this again. They are unlikely to find their previous home, unless it was quite close to you, but it will not stop them trying. Quite often the best solution to this problem is to contain the birds in your outside enclosure until they get used to their new surroundings. There is no hard and fast limit to how long you should do this before allowing them to free range. However, you would be strongly advised to do this for at least 6 weeks, preferably more

# 2) BUYING KEETS OR FERTILE EGGS FOR HATCHING

## A) WHERE CAN YOU BUY FERTILIZED EGGS FOR HATCHING?

You will no doubt find that suppliers of day old keets, will supply guinea fowl eggs for hatching. Suppliers will usually not offer guarantees that all eggs purchased will hatch. They will no doubt ensure to the best of their abilities that the eggs you purchase have been fertilized. The hatching of eggs is covered in detail in the section on breeding and hatching.

## B) HOW TO BEST START A FLOCK

Unless you have a particular desire to purchase a clutch of eggs and an incubator, then as a beginner the easiest route is to purchase a number of day old keets.

## C) WHERE TO BUY DAY OLD KEETS

Wherever you are located you should be able to find a local supplier, or at least one reasonably close that offers a delivery service. By doing a simple Google search for your area, you will no doubt find at least one suitable source.

### *Which hatchery should you go with?*

When buying Keets, a deciding factor of which hatchery you go with could be that many have a minimum order policy. Do not panic at the prospect of taking 20 keets when you only want 10. As mentioned previously, experienced keepers will often advise taking double the amount you need, partly because of aforementioned complications with keets dying. You will obviously do everything possible to ensure the survival of all the keets you buy. Simply by advertising or contacting a friend, you will no doubt find that you will have no trouble finding a new home for any surplus you have.

### Are day old keets and eggs available all year round?

Depending on demand you may also find that you cannot simply call a hatchery and get your keets straight away. You may in fact have to order in advance in say fall (autumn) for the following years delivery. If you are determined to get started with your keets as soon as possible, then this will probably be the deciding factor as to the hatchery you go with.

### Should you collect or have them delivered?

Suppliers of poultry usually have dedicated specialist courier services to handle delivery. If you are close enough to commute to a local supplier, be sure to take a suitable carrier for any day old keets. Depending on the number you purchase, a small cardboard box should be sufficient. Line the box bottom with a newspaper and soft shavings if you have them. Make sure the box has a lid to keep the keets warm until you get them home. It would also be preferable to take someone with you who can hold the box securely. Also ensure the box has some sort of ventilation, whether this is via the flaps of the lid or simply punching some holes into the box with a pen or pencil. On a particularly cold day, it would be advised to have the car heater running to ensure they don't become chilled. You should certainly not allow the keets to become chilled as they can easily become ill and die.

### Keets that die

Day old keets under any circumstances are at their most vulnerable in the first 10 days or so. It is unfortunate,

but do not be surprised if some of your keets die, either in transit or within the first few days or so. There can be all manor of reasons and it is not necessarily a fault of your own or an indication that the rest will soon expire.

## 3) WHERE TO BUY GUINEA FOWL

### Buying keets, adults or fertile eggs

Where will you buy your birds, or hatching eggs? In most cases local breeders exist worldwide, but if you decide to purchase a Vulturine or Crested variety, you may have to consider importation. Issues of quarantine will be observed as most countries look to control diseases. In modern times bird flu and other diseases can have devastating effects on all who come into contact. Positive testing in recent years has resulted in thousands of destroyed birds. However, the following website links cover a number of the available suppliers for both the USA and the UK.

This is not a definitive or exhaustive list and you are advised to search your local area for alternatives. A simple Google search for "*Guinea fowl [ your area ]*", will no doubt uncover quite a few more.

### A) US GUINEA FOWL SUPPLIERS:

Backyard Chickens is an excellent resource for both additional advice and Guinea Fowl for sale.

**Backyard Chickens**
*http://www.backyardchickens. com/f/45/guinea-fowl*

Guinea Farm are based in Iowa and again have hatching eggs and Guinea Fowl keets etc, at different stages.

## Guinea Farm

*http://www.guineafarm.com/*

Strombergs have a vast array of birds for sale as well as accessories.

## Strombergs Chickens

*https://www.stromberg-schickens.com/prod_detail_list/Peafowl-Guineas*

Efowl, again have a wide range of poultry types as well as accessories and housing.

## Efowl

*http://www.efowl.com/Guinea_Fowl_Breeds_for_Sale_s/58.htm*

Guinea Fowl International, offer a list of breeders in the U.S. at the following web address

## Guinea Fowl International

*http://guineas.com/breeders/*

Guinea Fowl Breeders Association again offers a list of breeders in the U.S.

## Guinea Fowl Breeders Association

*http://www.gfba.org/*

*Other breeders and suppliers available are as follows:*

## W R Hatchery

*http://wrhatchery.com/guinea-keets.html*

## Mail Order Poultry

*https://www.mailorder-poultry.com/product/french-guinea-keets/*

## Chickens Direct

*https://chickensdirect.net/poultry/french-guinea-keets/?gclid=Cj0KEQjwnrexBRDNmZzNkf7c4c4BEiQALnlx-hQ_RITUoPTHrq-mIHYny-fqnNCQF9moIGaEDTYcK-0bzsaApeT8P8HAQ*

## Brown Egg Blue Egg

*http://www.brownegg-blueegg.com/HatcheryLinks.html*

## Purely Poultry

*https://www.purelypoultry.com/guineas-c-257_157.html*

*Vulturine and Crested Guinea Fowl suppliers:*

As you can imagine Vulturines are not as readily available, but there are a few suppliers as follows:

## Purely Poultry

*https://www.purelypoultry.com/vulturine-guineafowl-p-923.html*

You may find the following useful and informative:

## Casuarius

*http://casuarius.webs.com/guineafowl.htm*

## Backyard Chickens

Have a useful thread that may be of use

*http://www.backyardchickens.com/t/248453/looking-for-vulturine-guinea-fowl-and-black-crested-guinea-fowl-sale*

## OLX,

At the time of press there were several Vulturine for sale. Of course these may not be available when you search.

*http://www.olx.co.za/q/fowl/c-811*

## b) UK GUINEA FOWL SUPPLIERS:

The following website provides a good list of Guinea Fowl suppliers in England, Wales, Scotland and Northern Ireland

*http://www.chickens.allotment-garden.org/poultry-suppliers/guinea-fowl-breeder-UK.php*

## Preloved

Is another good place to search for Guinea fowl keets, adult birds etc, that are currently available.

*http://www.preloved.co.uk/adverts/list?keyword=guinea fowl*

## Bird trader

has birds and fertile eggs advertised, and is well worth a look whilst researching

*http://www.birdtrader.co.uk/poultry-for-sale/guineafowls*

## UK Guinea fowl

Based in Devon and specialize in Ducks and Geese as well as Guinea Fowl. Guinea Fowl are generally available as follows:

## *Hatching Eggs:*

Available from April to the End of August

## *Day old keets,*

Poults as well as occasional surplus adult breeding stock.

They do offer delivery but not on certain items such as day old keets.

*http://ukguineafowl.co.uk/guinea-fowl/*

## Moon Ridge Farm

Again based in Devon sell a number of poultry varieties and wildfowl. Their Guinea fowl are also available as either eggs, day old keets, poults or adults.

Again, please check their current terms and conditions regarding delivery.

*http://moonridgefarm. co.uk/shop/guinea-fowl-pea- fowl/guinea-fowl/*

Other websites offering similar Guinea Fowl at different stages are as follows:

*http://www.cacklehatchery. com/guinea.html*

*http://www.irishfowl. com/irish-poultry-breeders. php?q=guinea&name=Guinea Fowl*

*http://www.guinea-fowl. co.uk/13-furtherinfo.html*

*http://www.henleechickens. co.uk/guinea-fowls-for-sale*

### *Vulturine and Crested Guinea Fowl suppliers:*

As you can imagine Vulturines are not as readily available, but there are a few suppliers as follows:

At the time of press there was only one UK supplier, however, please conduct your own Google search as these can occasionally be advertised on specialist, classified, bird sites.

**Pheasants UK**

*http://www.pheasants-uk. co.uk/price list.html*

Pheasants UK have both Vulturine and Crested Guinea Fowl listed, but you will have to check the price and availability of these.

# Chapter Four

# Housing Guinea Fowl

As previously mentioned, you will have no doubt considered the amount of space you actually have available. This chapter includes such things as bascic requirements for housing Guinea Fowl; where to site the building; the type of building you will need, and much more

## 1) IMPORTANT INITIAL CONSIDERATIONS

### *a) How much space do you have?*

PLEASE NOTE: Before undertaking any building/construction, check any permitted limits with your local council/authority.

Your options are only really limited to the space you have. If you can only partition the area in half, then this is better than not at all. But a larger area, perhaps an acre, will enable you to separate the area into quarters or more. More sections would mean you could separate the birds by age group, as well as a dedicated nursery/brooding area that is recommended anyway. If these are your first and only birds, then you would only perhaps need the brooding/nursery area that doubles into a hospital area for sick or injured birds.

Once you have measured the area that you would like to use and worked out how many birds you need, you then need to consider the type of enclosure required. We will go into much more detail about the details of area, units and bird numbers as we go, so do not worry about this for now.

### *b) Will you have to move the birds at any point?*

You need to be aware of the fact that if too many birds occupy a strip of land, the soil can become sour over time. This is usually as a result of overuse and too much nitrogen going into the ground from bird droppings. Grassy areas can become over grazed by birds and therefore unable to regenerate. Apart from problems with vegetation growth, sour ground can cause problems with disease. If you suspect that your soil may be suffering this condition, you may have to prevent any birds free ranging and therefore rest the area until it has time to recover. Some larger land owners rectify the problem by digging or ploughing the land over. Obviously what this means is that you will need an alternative area for the birds to free range. So again, when considering the area you have, do not just utilize one big area. You will probably be better to look at the area you have and then halve this, in case you have to leave an overused section to regenerate.

### c) Have the hen house and outside pen ready

Remember that you need to plan everything well in advance. The hen house and run should already be set up and ready to go. Once you decide that you intend to keep Guinea Fowl, start making plans for the accommodation. As previously mentioned there is much to consider and plan, such as how many you can accommodate and therefore what size of building you need. What you do not want is to order the day old keets and then have nowhere to house them after around 2 weeks in the brooder. In the case of incubating eggs, you have the best part of a month plus 2 weeks in a brooder. If you feel you can have the accommodation in place in around a week then by all means set up the brooder and order your keets. I would not advise working to a tight deadline and there are all manner of eventualities and things that you can easily miss. It is better to have this all in place ready to go. Remember that you need this housing and run safe and secure from predators and this part of the construction can be time consuming.

### d) What are the basic requirements for housing Guinea Fowl

Basically Guinea Fowl housing needs to be safe from predators. It should be dry, well ventilated but draft free. Have adequate roosting perches, preferably as high as you can make them. Ideally you should have some sort of insulation to protect the birds in freezing temperatures and not have the need to heat the building.

What you will need regardless of whether you are keeping them free range or otherwise, is a safe, secure place for them to roost. You will ideally shut and lock your birds away over night. The main reason for this is for protection against predators. The shelter would also protect the birds against adverse weather. With this in mind, the enclosure and housing needs constructed so that a fox or coyote would not be able to break in. It would also of course need to be rain and draught proof.

If you have an existing set up, perhaps because you have chickens, then you will base the number of Guineas you purchase, to the remaining space available. Again, we will go into more detail about the recommended size needed per bird.

### A shelter for adverse weather conditions.

Open fronted shelters are often recommended for Guinea Fowl to roost under as they generally prefer these to a closed shed, but are perhaps not suitable accommodation during adverse weather. This includes rain, heat (extreme sun), cold (frost and snow), wind (draughts and cold chills)

If you live in an area prone to heavy or prolonged rain conditions, then it is advisable to have appropriate shelter. As the birds need to scratch and dust bathe on a regular basis, this may mean that you have to make an indoor area for this purpose.

### Where to site buildings?

If it is possible, you should site buildings whereby the housing and outdoor pen receive the maximum amount of daily sun. This is particularly important during times when the birds need to be locked up during adverse weather conditions. If you are not sure, then I would suggest you spend a sunny day monitoring which areas get the most sun. Of course you may not have a choice in the matter if you are pushed for space. In which case, you simply have to erect the building where ever you can.

### So what kind of a construction do Guinea Fowl need?

The good news is that Guinea Fowl do not require any elaborate constructions. In fact the best solution to housing them is often to convert an existing building. This conversion can be as simple as four walls and an entrance door with sufficient perches for the birds to roost. Many poultry keepers have successfully converted an old garden shed or an old caravan. The important thing is that you incorporate perches as high as you possibly can, as Guinea Fowl prefer to roost in high spots.

### Suitable hen house/coop

It is not the purpose of this book to go into a lot of detail regarding hen house construction. There are many excellent resources and books available that cover this in great depth. It is a choice that you should make as to whether you buy something purpose built, make your own from scratch or convert an existing building. If it were myself with this choice, I would convert an existing suitable building. Suitable does not necessarily mean an existing brick built farm building such as a barn or cow shed. Suitable can mean an old lean-to or storage shed. As mentioned, many people convert old caravans or buses.

## _How big should the housing be?_

Apologies in advance for the mathematics here. But this will at least give you an idea of what you need to consider when working out as precisely as you can, how many birds will fit into the space you have. I have used the following, in the past for planning and constructing poultry buildings.

There are a number of opinions about how much space each bird needs whilst living in the coop. The following is the general theory that the author has picked up when working out numbers of birds for available space. They all more or less come back to the basic need for each bird that is approximately 2 to 4 square feet. This is not intended to be an exact science, but will give you a fairly accurate idea of how many birds you will comfortably accommodate in the coop you intend to have.

Once again, a good rule of thumb is that each bird should have around 2 to 4 square feet (0.2m² to 0.4m² approx) of space. That is 1ft x 2ft, or 2ft x 2ft. With a floor space of 6ft x 10ft (1.8 meters x 3 meters), if you opted for 1ft x 2ft you could accommodate 30 birds. If you decided 2ft x 2ft was more appropriate, this would accommodate 15 birds. The easy way to calculate this is to take the overall square foot area of the coop and divide this by the square footage needed per bird. So again, 6ft x 10ft = 60ft² is the overall square foot area. Divide that by 2 = 30, or 30 birds. Divide by 4 = 15, or 15 birds.

Taking another example of a 10ft x 12ft (3 meters x 3.7 meters approx) space, this would be 120ft². Divide that by 2 = 60, or 60 birds. Divide by 4 = 30, or 30 birds.

Please note, these are just suggestions and you should judge this for yourself, depending on how you will lay out the coop interior. Just remember, that not all of the birds will be scratching about on the floor at the same time. Some will be, but others will be on roosting perches. Also, other than at night, you are unlikely to have them locked up in the coop all the time. However, you need to factor in room taken up by nest boxes, feeders and drinkers and any other bulky item likely to take up space inside. In order to keep the floor space uncluttered, it will also be necessary to have raised nest boxes and hanging feeders. One of the best roosting perches is the ladder perch, which we will talk about later.

An even easier way to approach this, would be to start with for example, 10 birds and observe how they manage in that space. If there seems to be more than enough room and you are happy with that amount of birds then all well and good. If you think you could manage more birds then you can always add to this later.

Please do not ignore planning and measuring in this way. It is important as it assumes this gives each bird enough space to scratch and pick about the floor.

## 2) ADDITIONAL INFORMATION RELATING TO SUCCESSFULLY HOUSING GUINEA FOWL

### A) BEHAVIORAL PROBLEMS THROUGH OVERCROWDING

Overcrowding, whether this is free range or battery cages, can cause all manner of behavioral problems among birds. If they are not given enough space they can quickly become aggressive with pecking and fighting being common place.

Guineas or in fact any poultry, should not be confined for long, in small spaces such as cages. They need the freedom to move about and to roost. By confining the birds, you encourage hostile behavior such as feather pick-

ing, general pecking and fighting. It is for that reason that it is important to permit each bird a minimum space of approximately 2 ft$^2$ (0.18m$^2$ approx) to 4 ft$^2$ (0.37m$^2$ approx). Some insist that 0.4m$^2$ (4.3 ft$^2$) minimum is used. And yet some keepers would suggest 0.9m$^2$ of floor space is adequate per bird.

Even if your birds are free range or have use of a run/yard, it is important to be aware of space needed. This is particularly important because during bad weather, you will need to confine the birds to the house. Below we will go into much more detail about what space is necessary and recommended, as well as not recommended.

### B) MANAGING AVAILABLE SPACE

Perhaps the average keeper does not have to worry about maximizing yield, in the same way that a meat producer would. In other words making sure that each square foot of space is utilized to its maximum potential. However we can learn a lot from what producers consider to be necessary in terms of how much space the birds need and then adjust accordingly. Please do not assume I am encouraging intensive production, this is just for information purposes.

So in order for a farmer or other intensive producer, to remain sustainable over the years, they have to follow good management practices. If they failed to do this they would soon run into problems with disease and therefore reduced production. This would in turn defeat the whole object of them being in business.

On free range land, what can the keeper do to effectively manage space?

1. Rotation of usage each year is often the first consideration. This involves moving the entire flock to a new section of land and leaving the land fallow. If the sheds are moveable, then this often involves moving the sheds to the new area.

2. Removal of feces should be given a priority and it should not get to the stage where the birds are allowed to tread in it.

## Mezzanine floor space

Mezzanine floor space is often recommended as this allows you to get more birds into a smaller space. Mezzanine floors are basically an extra floor within a large building. The floor is usually one corner of a building with the raised floor being built on stilts or posts for support. Many factories and warehouses use these to good effect if they need to maximize floor space in one small area. This eliminates the need for storage shelves that are usually laid out in rows and require an aisle either side to allow a forklift truck access. It we take the example that our building is 12ft x 10ft x 7ft, we could use the mezzanine floor idea to accommodate nesting boxes and a nursery/brooding area. This would therefore mean that the birds would still have the same floor space available. In other words, you have a mezzanine floor in place, which would allow birds to actually walk about and scratch on the raised floor. Below this, you would have the nest boxes or brooding area, or just the existing floor space.

## Should you have an outside yard/run, and how big should this be?

It is recommended that the area of this run for several birds should be at least 3 meters x 7 meters. (9ft 10" x 23ft approx)

Once again the size of the yard should be measured in the same way as the coop, on a per bird basis. In other words, allow $2ft^2$ to $4ft^2$ ($0.2m^2$ to $0.4m^2$ approx) of space for each bird. But do not feel you have to stick to those dimensions, many keepers prefer to make this area bigger than the coop floor area. So for a 6ft x 10ft coop, you may prefer a 12ft x 10ft run. The coop size gives a reasonable amount of space for each bird in case you have to lock the birds up for a while during adverse weather conditions. The pen enclosure however, can be as big as you can manage. Baring in mind that you are trying to substitute total free range even if you cannot give the birds actual free range.

## 3) PREDATORS

As part of this section on accommodating your Guinea Fowl, special construction needs should be considered in terms of the problems associated with predators.

Predators can be a very big problem for Guinea Fowl. Some keepers would strongly assert that many more Guinea Fowl deaths occur from predator attacks than diseases.

### A) POSSIBLE PREDATORS OF GUINEA FOWL

Possible predators of Guinea Fowl include: bears, game hunters, mountain lions, eagles and other birds of prey, fox-

es, pet dogs and cats, raccoons, skunk, snakes and coyote. Of course this depends on where in the world you may be and at what age the Guinea Fowl are. Younger birds will be more vulnerable than wiser mature birds. In many cases the shriek of a number of Guinea Fowl can be quite intimidating to a possible predator, and make the predator think twice about attacking. Domesticated gun dogs, or collies could be a problem, as they have a natural tendency to stalk, hunt and in some cases kill game birds.

### B) Which predators and where are they?

Different predators inhabit different locations, and so it may be necessary to do your own research to ascertain this. Or you can search this or contact The U.S. Fish and Wildlife Service via the following website;

*http://www.fws.gov/*

They should be able to advise you specifically or at least point you in the right direction to find local organizations.

You ideally need this information because if flying predators are a problem, you definitely need a wire covered top. If it is digging predators, you will certainly have to safeguard your enclosure by digging below ground level and burying wire fencing. Of course there is nothing to stop you utilizing all of these preventative measures, just in case.

Digging predators include; wolverine, badgers, raccoons, wolf, opossum, skunk, lynx, weasel, mink, bobcat and snakes.

### C) Problems once predators attack

The main problem once a predator makes an attack is that they are likely to come back again. In some cases certain larger predators can wipe out a whole flock in a matter of hours. This is why you should take the time, effort and expense to properly secure your coop and outside run. Once again prevention is far far better than cure.

### D) ARE SOME PREDATORS MORE DANGEROUS THAN OTHERS?

Predators vary with how dangerous they are to Guinea Fowl and poultry in general. Predators such as foxes and coyote, will actively search out and kill adult birds and of course keets. Others such as weasels, stoats, mink, opossum, snakes, raccoons etc, may try to take keets, but will raid a nest for eggs. Guinea Fowl, particularly broody hens are likely to fight and fend off such predators. Unfortunately they are not likely to be successful against larger predators.

### E) PREDATOR DETERRENTS

In the wild Guinea Fowl are known to be extremely resourceful at evading predator attacks. This is probably due to the fact that they are more alert and wary of sudden movements or potential attacks.

Once the birds become domesticated however, they could fall prey to domesticated animals. This can occasionally happen if they are raised around domestic cats and dogs. There is the possibility that they may become confident around any domestic cat or dog and get too close. It would not take much for a dog or cat, with the intent to catch a Guinea Fowl, to make a lunge and grab one.

### Why do Guinea Fowl suddenly start calling out?

The shrieking alarm call that the Guinea Fowl make could very well scare a predator off. It could also have the detrimental effect of alerting predators to their presence, as a potential meal.

When you hear the Guinea alarm call, and they start shrieking, you may find that a predator is close by. Because of their naturally alert suspicious nature, it is not very often they will be caught by such predators. Once one Guinea Fowl starts, this alerts the others and they all call out. The noise can be understandably annoying, particularly

if it is persistent. You can of course sympathize when you understand that it is just their natural self preservation measure. They are of course not just looking out for themselves but everyone else, so you cannot blame them for this. If you keep chickens, they may not be as alert to predator dangers, and will certainly benefit from the ever present Guinea Fowl.

### Security lights as deterrents

You may have security lights set up on your property anyway. If you don't, I would strongly advise having either a permanent light overlooking their outside run, or at least a trip light or series of trip lights that will illuminate the area. This enclosure light can also be very useful when night time comes and some Guineas are still in the run roosting. You certainly do not want to leave them outside and so need to get them into the coop. You will find it a lot easier to get them into to the coop if there is a light in the run and the Guinea Fowl can see the door to the coop.

Also be aware that some digging predators such as opossums are very adaptable and can easily scale a fence and if you do not have the roof wired, can easily get into the enclosure.

### Dogs as deterrents

Many keepers do this with pet dogs that guard and patrol the property and will certainly act as a deterrent for most predators. Perhaps not bears or mountain lions.

### When predators become a problem

Sometimes you will spot a predator prowling about, not necessarily on or near your premises. In these cases I would strongly advise not allowing your flock to free range until you are sure the threat has gone. This may involve locking them up for a few day, a week or more.

If predators become a real problem to the welfare of your livestock, you may feel inclined to take matters into your own hands. In some areas, owning fire arms such as shotguns is permitted under license. However, you should not assume that the owning of them allows you to freely kill known predators. Birds of prey in particular can be very problematic as predators of livestock. But you will no doubt find they are protected, and it is therefore against the law to shoot and kill them. In all cases you need to check the law in your area regarding the killing of pests and predators. If you are found guilty of killing an animal that is protected by law, you may find yourself facing a hefty fine or even prison sentence. So please do check the law regarding such matters.

### Taking advice before taking matters into your own hands

You may also need to take advice as to how you can deal with the predator. In a lot of cases these animals are protected anyway and so you cannot just shoot a potential predator, nor should you be encouraged to do so. These are wild animals and are merely doing what any wild animal would do; looking for food. What you ideally need to do is discourage a predator from venturing onto your property.

**Protection from predators:** Consider an electric fence to deter larger predators from your boundary.

## 4) PROBLEMS WITH RODENTS

### A) RATS AND MICE

Rats and mice have always been considered a serious pest for a number of reasons. They can be prolific disease and pest carriers. They are extremely versatile and adaptable and will take up residence anywhere that they can gain access to. They will destroy and gnaw their way through cables, pipes, woodwork, cardboard, paper, clothing and this isn't always for nesting material. Nesting material as such is needed also, as they are prolific breeders. They will not only eat any available food, but may even kill baby keets and eat unprotected eggs.

### Fixing wiring

When you fix wiring to a pen, such as chicken wire, you need to ensure the joints are secure. A determined intruder will soon find any weak spots and force entry into your pen.

### Mice and chicken wire

You may have to consider using chicken wire to keep mice out if they become a problem. Be aware that mice are also known to have no problem getting through the narrowest of chicken wire. ½ cm approx (¼ inch approx), is not unusual for younger mice to squeeze through. You may therefore need to apply two layers with one hole overlaying the other, or just use wire with a narrower hole.

### Poison

Poison that you do use must be placed in areas that the birds cannot gain access to it. You must also check that there is nothing in the feed fed to your Guineas or other poultry that contains vitamin K. Past studies have shown that it can act as an antidote to certain poisons. So if rodents are eating any feed with vitamin K in, it will actually help them to eat the poison, without any ill effect.

# CHAPTER FIVE

# TYPES OF GUINEA FOWL HOUSING

The following offers the types of accommodation that have been typically used for Guinea Fowl, either for general keeping or farming and production.

## 1) ACCOMMODATION AND CONSTRUCTIONS

### *Farm Yard*

This will probably not be the sort of accommodation that most people will have access to, but is included as a possible alternative. In this case the birds have access to an open enclosure or run that is either grass, or a hard surface such as an impacted gravel yard or concrete. This is always more restricted than free range, but has many of the benefits. It is likely to incorporate a straw covered yard, aviary and a barn conversion.

The farm yard allows the birds freedom to roam, but may not have availability of vegetation and soil to scratch on.

### *Intensive*

Although intensive food production isn't the focus of this book much less space would be needed to keep a few hundred birds.

More for information purposes, intensive production will be discussed here.

Basically this involves utilizing a limited amount of space and stocking it with as many birds as is viable. It is not just a question of cramming a lot of birds into a small space. It requires a lot of preparation and management.

Nothing is taken to chance with these operations as there is usually a large capital outlay at stake. So this will include the basics such as automatic feeders and drinking stations. The correct number of birds for the space so they are not unnecessarily over crowded. Regular cleansing, disinfecting and litter replenishment, to avoid bacteria

build up and other diseases.

Buildings should be sufficiently heated and ventilated. However, if the temperature becomes greater than 86° F (30° C), then more ventilation will be required. It is usually necessary to achieve this mechanically with a fan unit.

In a lot of cases the shavings are usually topped up so that there is a dry top layer at all times. The buildings are then cleaned out several months later, usually with a digger or tractor, as this would be very labor intensive.

Intensive farming of Guinea Fowl has become popular in line with their popularity as a meat product. Guinea Fowl have been farmed for centuries and demand has increased over recent years across Europe and USA.

In this respect, birds are kept on a large scale in very controlled but intensive environments. Birds are kept either in cages or open plan deep litter buildings. They are also successfully kept in semi intensive set ups. This combines both intensive housing with free range. As you may expect, a great deal of research and development has been involved with the aim to produce a bird that has an optimum yield over the shortest period of time.

### *Battery cages*

There has been much controversy over the years concerning the health and welfare of battery hens. The keeping of birds in an intensive system is something that many people oppose for obvious ethical reasons. It is usually when certain producers have been exposed for not following standards of care that are supposed to be adhered to, but in some cases, are not. Unfortunately there are cases of abuse and neglect, but more often than not, animals are kept in line with regulated standards.

This is still practiced but in a more humane way, than previously. Birds that are kept in cages, which is not a common practice for Guinea Fowl, are closely regulated to ensure standards are met. Guinea Fowl are not as docile as chickens, and are generally not seen as suitable for such confinement. An obvious problem with intensive keeping, particularly in cages is the risk of brittle bones and loss of muscular definition. For obvious reasons, the birds are not able to exercise and so can develop wasting diseases.

Intensive rearing of Guinea Fowl is therefore usually restricted to large open plan spaces, similar to the barn system.

Incidentally eggs for sale in supermarkets are now commonly labeled as either free range or from hens confined to battery conditions.

### Intensive barns, deep litter, cages

These buildings are generally purpose built with controlled facilities. The buildings are constructed to either allow natural ventilation or controlled with fans. Food and water is automatically administered

Water would be pipe fed with automatic drinkers. Food may well be conveyed automatically to the birds. The obvious advantage of this is that it is very labor saving. The average keeper is unlikely to have enough birds to warrant this kind of a set up. But if you keep only a few birds, you will know how much time it takes you to fill feeders, and water dispensers, not to mention clear out manure regularly.

A) PROBLEMS WITH KEEPING BIRDS INDOORS

Birds that are kept indoors on deep litter beds are more likely to experience disease problems if the litter is allowed to become and stay damp. Warm, damp, feces stained litter will not only promote respiratory problems but also encourage lice, mites and other parasites to thrive. You will notice you have a potential problem waiting to happen if you smell ammonia. Prevention is always better and easier than cure. You should therefore keep all areas as clean and dry as possible.

B) KEEPING THE LITTER DRY

Bedding should be kept as dry as possible and if necessary muck the birds out as often as possible. As previously noted, deep litter beds work well provided they are regularly topped with dry shavings. Whether you use shavings, straw or sawdust, the last thing you want is for this to remain damp. If everything, including droppings is kept as dry as possible, then the likelihood of bacteria, pests and disease is greatly reduced. Also bear in mind the absorbency of bedding such as straw. This can easily become and retain damp. Mold can quickly develop and in a damp environment, cause respiratory problems.

C) SEMI-INTENSIVE

For the enthusiast/general keeper, a much better compromise can be found with a semi free range. In this case the birds do not have the luxury of roaming at will. They do however have the fresh air and natural foraging, but in a fully enclosed pen or aviary. Provided the birds are not over crowded, they will happily go about their business.

## D) FREE RANGE

*Free range housing*

Free range housing usually allows

Free range is perhaps the best method as this suits the Guinea Fowls natural semi wild tendency. However for free range to be successful, you need sufficient space.

### What is free range?

Free range systems usually include a large area of open pasture, that is fenced off to some extent. The birds are then basically let out of their housing enclosure in the morning, then rounded up and locked up in the evening.

Free range by definition is the keeping of any animal under natural organic conditions. It suggests that the animal has the freedom and space of movement that is as close to their natural wild habitat as possible.

the birds plenty of room to move about, roost and scratch the ground. Sometimes it is necessary to keep the birds locked up, if weather conditions are particularly bad.

As you know, overcrowding is fraught with possible problems. It is therefore important that you plan accordingly to ensure that you make the best use of the space you have.

### Total free range (roaming free)

However some keepers of Guinea Fowl, particularly on large farms and estates prefer to allow the flock to roam at will. In such cases, providing the birds have plenty of natural shelter, housing may be deemed unnecessary. They will often prefer to roost in trees and forage for insects etc. Supplementary food can be given, but often they will get most of their food in the natural surroundings. This situation is as close as the birds are likely to come to living wild.

### What is the best land to use for free range?

It is unlikely that you would consider using prime arable land for free range birds. So generally the land used would be of a lesser quality but suitable for grazing. You would certainly not be advised to consider land that has been used for industrial purposes containing toxins or such like.

### Condition of the land

The ideal land conditions for poultry such as chickens and Guinea Fowl, would be dry and well drained. So sites that are in an 'at risk area' of flooding would not be suitable. Heavy clay land that typically does not drain well would also not be viable. Land such as this is at risk of becoming muddy with constant treading. It may be possible to add extra drainage to the land, and as long as it was cost effective, then this could be a remedy for bad draining land.

### Does the free range land have access to services?

In general most people considering establishing a free range system are likely to have land attached to their property. However, some people might be considering a free range, or perhaps semi intensive system, that is in an adjacent or remote area. So for someone planning to acquire land for free range purposes will need to address the following:

Check that the land has access to services such as a water and electricity supply. Pipe work for water needs to be

adequately insulated in case of freezing. You may need to have an alternative water source such as a pond, lake, stream or river. This will be an emergency back-up in case of freezing, or water supply being temporarily unavailable for whatever reason. It may also be necessary to have a generator on hand in case of an electricity power cut.

### How many birds should be kept free range?

Opinions differ as to how many birds should be kept on a per acre basis. Some suggest that approximately 100 birds should be kept on 1 acre of land. Other opinions on this are that on the same size land, around 300 birds could be kept in a semi intensively managed system.

### Recommended area

Again a recommended area for approximately 100 birds is an area of 7m x 8m x 1.5m high (23ft x 26ft x 5ft approx). This should have a sloping roof, of marine ply and felting or something similar. You will probably notice that using our previous calculations of each bird requiring between 2 and 4 square foot, that 100 birds is not a lot. However, total free range is supposed to allow more space and again this is only a guideline.

### What is the ideal size needed

It is debatable what is the ideal area that should be used for each bird. If you have an area of land that you would like to dedicate to keeping poultry then you will no doubt wish to maximize this to its full potential. Some keepers will say that as an example a 50ft x 50ft area i.e. 250 square foot of space would be ideal for 25 birds. This would give each bird 10 square foot of space each or an area of 2ft by 5ft, which as you can see is a generous amount per bird. Some keepers would even suggest that 50 birds could be accommodated on the 250 square foot of space. This is obviously a matter of opinion, and whether this causes behavioral problems because of overcrowding.

Some would suggest that a size 80 feet by 35 feet (24.4 meters by 10.7 meters) would be ample space for around 30 birds. This is approximately 260 m$^2$ (2798.6 ft$^2$), so if we divide that by 30, each bird should be allowed approximately 8 m$^2$ (86 ft$^2$ approx) or an area of 4 meters by 2 meters (13 ft by 6.5 ft approx) for each bird. As you can see, that is considerably greater. When deciding space issues, a lot depends on the welfare of the animal. However, birds still have adequate space, given 2 to 4 feet squared.

### Advantages for farmers of free range birds

There are also a lot of free range producers that take advantage of the free range products that have an increasing demand from the consumer.

Free range products also tend to attract a greater return. In that respect a lot of people are prepared to pay the extra premium knowing they are buying products from animals kept under more natural conditions.

Free range systems do not incur the vast capital costs associated with more intensive systems. Capital costs such as plumbing, cages and other fixed costs. This includes many variables such as electricity for heating, lighting, ventilation etc.

### Disadvantages for farmers of free range birds

Free range systems tend to be more labor intensive in comparison to the more automated battery style systems or semi intensive. The latter systems are likely to utilize automatic feeders and drinkers. Free range on the other hand will need people to actually fetch and carry food and perhaps water, if automatic drinkers are not in place.

### Advantages of woodland free range

In wooded areas such as orchards, the trees will shade and protect grass areas that would otherwise quickly dry and wither in hot exposed areas.

### Are the birds better off on free range?

A big plus point for free range birds is that they are a lot less susceptible to disease. No doubt this has much to do with the fresh air they receive, as well as additional nutrients and minerals they are picking up.

### E) PROBLEMS WITH FREE RANGE

### Drainage issues

Land that has to be reused or is bad draining, you can cultivate or plough. Alternatively, you can dig a pit up to 8inch (20 cm) and fill with hard-core and sand, before adding the top soil, at least 4 inch (10 cm). As the Guinea Fowl do not scratch very deep this should not be a problem.

### Re-seeding

If you have to re-seed, then the following would be recommended, and preferably as a mixture to add variety; rye grass, red and white clover, rape seed, cocksfoot grass or fescue grass.

### Land Problem areas

The land also needs to be able to support vegetation growth, so hot dry areas may also prove problematic for free range birds.

You would have to supplement the birds lack of natural food and also risk the birds leaving in search of a suitable food source.

### Land usage

It is usually necessary to rest or leave dormant land that has been well used throughout the year. If space is limited, then it may be necessary to partition off the outside pen. The land needs to be free from disease and pests and ideally, have healthy growing vegetation. This is either grass or wild herbs, clover, chickweed etc, that you cultivate for the benefit of the Guinea Fowl or other poultry.

### Remedy for sour ground

Land that has a burnt grass look or sour land, may need to be turned over using either a plough or using a cultivator such as a 2 wheel tractor. Once this is done, if you wished to keep the area grassed, it would be necessary to re-seed this and allow it to re-grow. It would therefore be necessary to keep the area clear, as the Guinea Fowl would eat the new shoots, before they had time to develop. If there is no new growth, then there may be a more serious problem, and the ground may need soil testing.

### Leaving land fallow

The important thing is that the rested area is kept fallow preferably for at least 12 months, but at least for as long as healthy growth is evident.

### Fallow land and treating

Areas that are left fallow should be treated in some way. Lime was traditionally used as a disinfectant, but suitable chemicals are available to do the same job.

### Land rotation system

Many poultry keepers advocate having a rotation system, whereby an area is left fallow for 6 months or more. If you search suppliers of poultry housing you will see small units that have a house and run attached in one. These are ideal if you have 2 or 3 birds and an area of grass land. You leave the birds in one area for a few weeks or months, and when the birds have grazed most of the grass, you move the unit to a fresh area. This is a perfect preventative solution to any future sour land problems. The only problem is if you have a bigger unit and moving it becomes impractical. There is also the risk of the less permanent structures been easier to break into by predators.

F) AVIARIES OR OTHER EN-CLOSURES.

The birds are obviously limited to the confines of the area they forage in. In the wild or a large free range area, they would have unlimited choice. In an enclosure you may have to provide them with a large area that has a lot of naturally growing vegetation and insects. But this is unlikely to provide them with the same amount of natural feed as free range. You therefore have to be more discerning and make sure you are giving the birds the necessary requirements. You will obviously be able to provide pellet feed ad lib, but you will have to ensure they get sufficient green vegetation on a daily basis.

### *Does the type of system affect meat production?*

Again the following will probably not be of interest to the reader unless you are planning to produce Guinea Fowl for meat/table purposes. There does not seem to be much difference in the size of a meat bird produced with either system. However the more intensive systems tend to produce the birds at a faster rate than the free range.

There does seem to be a lot of pros and cons to each system. At the end of the day, as long as there is a demand for any product, the product will be produced. Additionally, as long as the consumer requires a cheaper product, produced faster, then the supplier will seek to make this as cost effective as possible.

## 2) PRELIMINARY CONSIDERATIONS FOR THE HOUSING/ CONSTRUCTION.

**Lighting:** Electricity can be fed to the hen house by either having cables permanently installed or running an extension lead. It is your choice as to which you prefer. If you intend to build a place that houses your poultry as well as accommodates a brooder, incubator and acts as a store area for food and eggs etc, then you may need to think about a permanent installation. The main considerations are, that a brooder will need a heat lamp and obviously an incubator needs an electrical source. Some keep-ers insist that a light with a low watt-age light bulb is kept on overnight, so that the birds can see what is going on around them. If the temperature drops significantly low, then you are likely to need some sort of heat source.

**Ventilation:** The whole point of ventilation in a hen house is to ensure that fresh air from outside is circulated inside. Free range keepers generally find that as their birds are regularly exposed to fresh air, they suffer few if any diseas-es, in particular respiratory. Birds kept largely in poor housing with inadequate ventilation conversely experience greater health problems. In a badly ventilated area as the birds breathe, they are taking in anything airborne. This can include bacteria, viruses, mold spores, high dust, carbon dioxide build ups to name but a few.

**Temperature:** In most cases, tem-perature only becomes a problem in ex-tremes. In other words if you live in a relatively hot or cold part of the world, or at least areas that become periodically hot or cold. If an artificial heat source is needed, you should always consider an electrical appliance. You should certainly never consider gas or paraffin heaters for example. Apart from the obvious fire risk, particularly if kept running over night, there is also a risk of carbon monoxide poisoning

## 3) CONVERTING AN EXISTING BUILDING:

### A) INSULATING AND BOARDING THE PLACE OUT.

If you were to convert an exist-ing building you may want to consider lining this out with ply board sheets. Particularly if the building is old and draughty, you will mask the whole area. By being relatively air tight this will also block any mouse holes. Some would suggest that you do not want to insulate any cavities this new cladding creates. I personally would suggest insulating as the building will be a lot warmer as a result. Admittedly there is the risk that using insulation will create an ideal habitat for mice and rats to set up home. Secondly the insulation could have the effect of keeping a build up of moisture in the enclosure. However, providing the building is ventilated this should not happen. As far as the cavities are concerned, mice would probably get in there anyway. One solution to this problem is to first of all line the boards with chicken wire, so the mice and certainly not rats, could get into the cavity. You may think this is a lot of trouble, but these preventative measures are generally well worth it in the end. But again the choice is yours.

Ultimately drafts and damp should be avoided as they are a major cause of respiratory illnesses for poultry.

## 4) CONVERTING A SHED

When planning for the whole unit, i.e. the housing and run, there are a number of choices that you should consider.

1. How many birds you intend keeping is obviously something you will have considered by now. This will obviously depend on any existing poultry such as chickens that you may already have. If you have chickens already, you will know how much space they ideally need. You will therefore have a pretty good idea of how many Guinea Fowl you will be able to accommodate. If you are starting from scratch with Guinea Fowl as your first and only poultry, then use the guidelines given to establish how big an area you have and therefore how many birds you can accommodate.

2. Do you intend to hatch your own keets from eggs or buy day old? (both options are preferable to buying mature birds)

3. If you are hatching your own or buying day old keets, and you have other mature poultry, you are advised to accommodate the brooder in the hen house. So is your shed/coop big enough to accommodate this. The brooder ideally needs to be inside a cubicle/pen, which can be in the corner of the hen house.

If you are converting a shed, the shed will probably be an empty space inside, with a door and windows pre-fitted. The first thing you should do is to make the building initially habitable. This will involve putting up perches, this will be covered later. You will also need to have in place food and water containers.

## 5) THE OUTSIDE RUN/YARD

As you already know, the run is necessary as it provides a free range environment in a relatively enclosed area. The birds ideally need, exercise, fresh air and the opportunity to forage for extra natural vegetation and other supplements.

Remember that your aviary construction or hen house and run, are likely to be permanent. Therefore this planning stage is very important. Outside pens should ideally be covered with 1 cm (½ inch square approx) chicken wire, which should prevent small pests from entering the area. Perhaps cheaper plastic mesh, that is now widely available, would provide a good option if you have to cover the roof of the pen. But maybe not so much lower down, where mice will easily chew through this. This will also prevent certain wild birds from entering. You may wonder what harm they can do? Well other than eating any food available, which can prove costly, they are also potential carriers of parasites and disease.

### a) Partition run

If you have the space to do so, a useful addition to any free range system, is to partition areas with wire fences or netting. This would mean they benefit from being in the fresh open air, but you can keep certain groups separate. Even if the majority of the pen is all open free range, you may wish to have a separate pen outside for sick or injured birds. It is also a good idea to have a separate section for a hen and keets to benefit without being bullied by older birds. If birds are separated like this and birds try to fight each other through the wire, then it will be a good idea to put barriers such as 2 ft boards, so they cannot see each other.

### b) How high should the fence of the run be?

It is recommended that the fence height is at least 6ft (1.8 meters approx) high. but taller if possible. If the area you are is exposed to high winds, you may need to offer screening, surrounding partially or totally. Alternatively sheltered areas should be available where the birds can escape any severe cross winds.

### c) Do you need to cover the top of the run?

Depending on the area you live and whether you can allow the birds to free range, will determine whether you cover the whole of the enclosure with wire or allow the roof to be open. If you wish the entire pen to be secured and therefore keep the poultry in the pen all the time, you simply wire over the roof. If you intend the roof to be open, you should ideally have landing boards running around the top of the fence. The birds will easily land on the top of the fence without, but these just make getting in and out easier. They should be about 12" (30.5cm) wide by whatever lengths are available. These can easily be screwed mid way to the timber running along the top of the fence.

### d) Using netting or wire to cover the run

For free range enclosures incorporating netting is certainly advisable as this prevents the birds flying over, or a bird of prey flying in. It is also a cheaper alternative to a permanent wire covering.

However, predators could easily break through the netting and so you need to be especially careful, to make the hen house secure.

## 6) CONSTRUCTING AN OUTSIDE RUN (EXTENSION TO THE HEN HOUSE)

Now that we have talked about the various aspects of the outside run, we will now cover the construction. As we have already mentioned, the outside pen/ enclosure should be as large as you can accommodate. You should at least make the height 6 foot (1.8m). This is as much for your benefit to comfortably move inside, when feeding or mucking out. You should take care that the construction for this uses strong materials. Timber should be used for the framework that is at least 3 inch by 2 inch (7.6cm x 5.1cm). Once you have your hen house in place, the pen would naturally be attached to that, at the same height and width. You could simply start by attaching 3 x 2 timber around the front edge of the hen house. That is a timber running down both sides and one across the top.

This would act as the anchor point to attach the pen to the hen house. The construction then consists of a series of posts around the perimeter of the pen, at approximately 6 foot (1.8m) intervals. The posts could be 3 inch by 2 inch (7.6cm x 5.1cm) thickness, but preferably 3" x 3", or even 4" x 4" would be better.

In order to retain a straight line you should attach a line to the edge of the shed and take this to the furthest point of the run. Once you are happy that the line runs flush with the shed, at a 90°angle to the front, you can set your first corner post. You then do the same to the other side, and then you have your basic perimeter.

### Concreting the posts

You should not concrete these posts in until you are certain that they do in fact run flush with the hen house. These posts can then be concreted in, by digging a hole at least 1ft (30.5 cm) deep, packing with hard core and finally pouring concrete in to seal it. It is best to leave these initial corner posts to set over night. You may wish to cover the posts with plastic sheeting to make them waterproof. Obviously you do not want the wooden posts to rot and so some sort of protection is definitely advisable. Some people prefer using actual concrete posts, approximately 1 meter high. These are concreted into the ground and act as an anchor, that you then bolt the timber posts to.

What you need to be aware of at this point, is that the height of each post is the same. This is not easy, particularly if your land is uneven. What I would personally do is to measure the posts so that once they are buried at least 1 ft deep, they are still higher than the coop. Once the posts are concreted in, what you will find is that some are higher than others. Once you are ready to attached the top beam that runs parallel to the ground, you can do these in sections and use the spirit level to guide you. When you have the first beam fixed, you then fix the next, again ensuring this is level, and so on. What you should then have is a line that runs from the coop to the farthest post that is level. You then simply cut any lengths that stick out above the beam.

### Other fence posts

Using a line (string, rope or builders line), run this from one side of the housing right around the first post and the second post, to the other side of the housing. You can then simply fill in the rest of the posts at 6ft intervals until you have a series of upright posts. Again concrete in as before and leave these to set over night.

## Making the frame of the fence

Once the concrete posts are set, you then simply nail or screw 3 inch by 2 inch (7.6cm x 5.1cm) timber to the top of each upright fence post. Make sure you use a spirit level to get the timbers level. This also applies to the upright posts. It not only makes the structure look professional and pleasing to the eye, but ensures the structure is sturdy This creates a sturdy frame for the roof. You would then need to attach timber that runs all the way round and approximately 1ft (30.5 cm) from the ground. You may then decide to do the same one foot from the roof level to add extra strength and stability.

## Doorway to the enclosure

What you then need to consider either at the end of the run or somewhere on either side is a main door way into the enclosure. This should be at least ideally 3ft (0.9 meters) wide, and will allow you to walk into the enclosure carrying a bucket at your side. It should also be wide enough that you can easily push a wheel barrow in, for clearing out manure or any other objects. The doorway will also ideally need a head height of at least 6 foot (1.8 meters approx) Where ever you create this door frame, you will probably have to cut the cross sections out and sink two more posts. You then

construct a timber frame to fit this.

## Attaching wire to the frame

Once you are happy that the frame is in place, you then need to attach strong gauge wire sheets to the frame. You need to bear in mind that the object of the wire is not only to keep the birds in, but most importantly keep predators out.

## Gauge thickness for a wire fence

Wire for the fences should be sufficiently thick gauge wise depending on the predator threat. A 13 gauge wire would be strong enough to keep out most likely predators such as fox and coyote. These usually come in rolls or sheets that you attach with either nails or heavy duty staples. Some people prefer a thicker gauge, perhaps 19 gauge, which has a thickness approximately 1 mm. There are many useful guides on the Internet describing how to attach chicken wire to posts, such as the following: http://homeguides.sfgate.com/attach-chicken-wire-posts-74974.html

## 7) KEEPING PREDATORS OUT

### A) SECURING THE ENCLOSURE

It is important from a predator point of view, to secure the enclosure. Bear in mind that many predators can and will dig under a fence into the enclosure. If they manage to dig under and get to the Guinea Fowl, or any poultry, the enclosure will do nothing but help the fox, coyote or whatever to kill the lot. Of course if you are around to hear the commotion, the Guinea Fowl will soon alert you. But such predators do not need a great deal of time to kill and so you have to act quickly.

If you do have potential ground digging predators in the surrounding areas you will need to use a wire or steel mesh barrier. Depending on the size of the predator, heavy duty steel mesh, is likely to keep out the largest digging predator. For snakes and rats etc, ¼ inch hardware cloth (which if you do not know, is like chicken wire sheeting, but smaller holes), is probably all that is necessary. Hardware cloth is also good for the bottom part of the fencing. It will at least stop rodents such as mice from walking through the fence, but unfortunately will not stop them climbing. If you can afford it then having some sort of heavy duty fencing and then covering entirely with hardware cloth, will keep out all predators with perhaps the exception of a grizzly bear.

### Keeping predators out

Even domestic dogs, will attempt to dig under the wire fence. As a safety precaution, you are advised to dig a trench into the soil at least 1 ½ feet (46 cm approx) deep and wide. What you are aiming to do is to bury the fence below ground level. The section that you bury should preferably be plastic coated to prevent corrosion. The reason you make the trench 1 ½ foot wide is that you need to bend a section of wire fencing at a 90°angle. This then sits in the bottom of the trench parallel to the ground. The remainder of the fence then runs up to ground level. You can then attach this to the rest of the fence above ground. This needs to be completed for the whole of the perimeter. The buried section and the perimeter section above ground, should form an L shape, but in reverse, so the base of the L runs on the outside of the perimeter fence. You then back fill the trench, packing this well in.

A lot of gardeners have been known to adopt this method to keep rabbits out. The rabbit will reach a fence and easily burrow a hole under. Horticulturists in the past have dug a trench between 0.3 to 0.5 meters approx, (12 inches and 20 inches approx) deep and the same wide. They then measure twice the length, e.g. 40 inches and then bend this at 20 inches at a 90° angle. Again, the section of wire sheet that you bury, forms an L shape. This is then buried into the ground. Incidentally this section should ideally be plastic coated to avoid rusting. In our example, the rabbit then comes to the perimeter of the fence, burrows down and hits the fence at a dead end. Hopefully the pest doesn't have the foresight to try again but digging over 0.5 meter away from the fence and over 0.5 meters down. It is unlikely but it can happen with other predators, that perhaps evade your trap by accident.

### B) AN ALTERNATIVE DIGGING PREVENTION

Obviously in this case rabbits are not really the problem, but foxes, coyotes and stray dogs could well be a problem. A concrete base could work just as well, whereby you dig a pit of perhaps a foot deep. You then take the wire fence to the 12 inch (0.3 meter approx) depth. Next you lay concrete at approximately 6 inch (15 cm approx). The fence is also concreted into the base, thus sealing it into the base. Once dry you fill the area with approximately 6 inch (15 cm approx) of soil, to give the birds their natural scratching area, and for vegetation growth. You could do the same thing by replacing the concrete with a complete wire sheet that covers the whole area, in this case you may only have to excavate to 6 inch (15 cm approx), but the sides of the fence that are buried i.e. at a depth of 6 inch, will need to be secured firmly to the wire base that you are burying. Ultimately it depends on which method is more practical and cheaper for you. This may all sound like a lot of work, but if you intend to keep your Guinea Fowl, or any other poultry you have, safe from predators, your hard work will pay off.

### c) Converting Flooring in the coop to keep predators out.

Care must also be taken with the choice of flooring in the coop. If you suspect that a predator can dig under the housing and break its way in, you should take precautions. If your existing building is of a brick or concrete construction, it is likely that the floor is concreted. However if your housing is a wooden construction, you need to make sure that this is as equally strong as the rest of the building. This may involve lining the floor with tough ply-board or even laying a concrete base yourself. Many keepers also take the precaution of burying a plastic coated heavy gauge wire mesh sheet. This is particularly useful if the building is placed directly on soil. As long as the wire sheet is secured to the actual building, this effectively creates a complete sealed box. If a predator tries to dig under the housing, they should not be able to get any further than the wire flooring.

## 8) Perches

### a) Roosting perches

Again, the perches should be as high as the coop permits. But if size and space is an issue they should be at least 50 to 60 cm from the ground. You can used 2 inch x 2 inch (5cm x 5 cm) timber with the edges rounded or 2" x 2" (5cm x 5 cm), doweling or even brush handles.

There are a number of options for perches, and this will depend on the size of the building. If you only have a few birds, one or two simple rails attached to the inside wall of the building will suffice. As well as using 2 inch by 2 inch (5.1 cm x 5.1 cm) timber with the edges rounded, you could use suitable branches of a similar dimension.

To fix the perches, you can either buy 90°angle brackets, usually used for shelving, or make a similar bracket yourself with suitable timber. You would only need a couple of 1foot lengths of 2" x 1" (5.1 cm x 2.5 cm) timber. You simply screw or nail two ends creating a 90°angle. You then measure the distance between and cut a third length that you screw or nail to the other two end pieces, thus forming a triangle.

You then attach the two angle supports to the wall. The distance between the supports should be the length of the timber perch, less approximately 6" (15.3 cm) at each end. This leaves a 6" (15.3 cm) overhang at each end.

### b) Dropping boards

If you use single perches, then it is a good idea to attach dropping boards under the perches. These can be approximately one foot wide and attached in the middle directly below the actual perch. The distance from the perch to the dropping board only needs to be approximately 1ft (30.5 cm). The effect of this is that which ever way the birds roost any droppings drop onto the board and are easily cleaned off, thus leaving the main floor clean of droppings.

Space needed: Allow approximately 0.9 sq meter to 1.2 sq meters (3 or 4 square foot) of space for each bird. However, some breeders suggest, with the ladder perch, each bird sat on a perch, could be allocated about 20 cm (8 inch approx).

The birds need to be able to move about freely, thus avoiding aggressive behavior associated with overcrowding.

### c) Converting a ladder perch

If you have sufficient room inside the hen house, another good roosting apparatus is a ladder perch. By its very name these are similar in design to a normal ladder, however they should be much wider. Again you should construct these with 2" x 2" timber with the edges rounded. At least 3ft (92 cm approx) wide and perhaps 6ft (184 cm approx) wide, should be a good guide.

To construct, measure from one ceiling corner, at an angle of approximately 45° to the floor. You may even have a suitable length of timber that you can offer up and use this as a guide. Once you have established the length, cut another length the same size. You then need a series of lengths that act as the steps. Again these should be somewhere between 3ft and 6ft (92cm and 184cm). You then space these at approximately 1 to 1.5 ft (30.5 cm to 46 cm) gaps, from one end to the other. Drill and screw or nail each step to the inside of the upright. When you have filled the length, you should have something resembling a wide ladder. You then place this at an approximate 45°

angle to the wall and preferably attach it at the top and bottom, to prevent it moving and possibly collapsing. You could also make a temporary attachment or hinge, that allows you to move the whole frame, for easy cleaning. The birds can then choose where they roost. However, unless you keep chickens as well, most guineas will prefer to roost as high as possible on the highest rungs. Although not an ideal roosting solution, it does offer an excellent space saving alternative to high perches along the walls.

You can also make a portable step roost if you do not wish to make the fixture permanent and are not sure exactly where to put it for best. These can be bought or made on a DIY basis. It is constructed in a similar way to a normal household wooden stair case. You have the base and the back and the steps would just be normal roosting perches. The easiest way to construct these is in the same way as the ladder perch. The only difference is that you do not attach this to a wall, but make it free standing, by again constructing a base and back, to form a triangle. You will then be able to move these where ever you like. It is best not to make these too big, and maybe best to have several. You want to make these easy and practical to move around.

Flat board roosts are also a very good option for the birds, particularly when the weather is cold or frosty. The board needs to be about 6 inches (15 cm approx) wide. The advantage of a flat board is that the birds feathers can cover its feet, and prevent frost bite. Again look at constructing these as above, but this time, more like an actual staircase. These can be either permanent or portable.

One other important point, is that you should avoid placing roosting perches near food or water outlets. For obvious reasons, droppings will soon make their way into the food and water and create a contamination risk

### d) Making a pit to collect droppings

You may find after a while that whichever type of perch you use, you will have to take measures to collect the droppings. If you use the ladder method, this could be a wire covered pit that the droppings fall into, or simply making sure that there is enough litter to absorb the droppings. I prefer a wire enclosed pit as this allows a build of dropping, but the birds are not walking in the droppings. Again you can make a framed box that has a ply base, and a timber frame approximately 1 to 1.5 ft (30.5 cm to 46 cm) high. This needs to slot under the ladder frame. You then cover the box with strong wire sheets, that allow the birds to walk on if they wish, but keeps their feet clean. If some birds prefer to roost on this wire pit whilst birds are roosting above, there is a risk they will have droppings land on them. This is not a big problem, but you may wish block access directly under the perch, with either a board or wire sheet.

### e) Raised wire floors

Some keepers also like to have raised housing with wire floors that the birds walk on. The advantage of this is any droppings fall through the wire floor, into a pit below. This keeps the birds clean, and the pit can be cleared whenever there is a sufficient build up. The disadvantage of this, is that if not properly boxed in, it could create an adverse draft. Also if it is possible for any predator to gain access, they could also break into the hen house, and probably kill all of your birds. If you do decide to utilize a wire floor, ensure that it is a strong gauge that would make it very difficult for even a large predator to break through.

### f) Perches and clipped wings

Birds that have clipped wings should be able to reach perches that are no more than 1.5 meters (5ft approx) high. If you notice the birds struggle trying to fly up to this height, then you will have to move the perches to 1 meter (3ft 3 inch approx) high, which they should have no problem with. This is another advantage of using a ladder perch, as the birds can move up to a higher perch in stages.

## 9) OTHER CONSIDERATIONS FOR THE COOP AND YARD

### Trees and shrubs in the pen

If your pen enclosure is big enough, it may be a good idea to introduce natural trees and shrubs. Trees and shrubs that are native to your area are often readily available in garden centers. A lot of natural hedging trees and bushes are ideal. So Hawthorn, Rowan, Bramble, Ivy, Holly, Cotoneaster and long wild grasses are a possibility. If you introduce natural cover, then the Guinea hen herself may be encouraged to dig a nesting hollow in a secluded area, lay and brood her own eggs.

### Outdoor perch

An outdoor perch although not vital would be a definite advantage to the birds. Some people make what is known as an A frame, which is like two ladder frames joined to form an A. You could also have a series of branches attached perhaps in each corner.

### Having two separate hen houses and run.

A good alternative would be to go back to our original plan of the permanent building. If you had sufficient land you could create a second run adjacent to the building. In other words you have the one hen house and two runs side by side. Or perhaps build a second housing with its own run on a separate part of your property. This could still be used as a storage area, but as long as you keep it free from poultry use. Then when you are ready to rotate your birds, you simply transfer them to the spare unit and leave the previous unit to rest.

### Advantages of a separate unit

The separate unit can also be very beneficial when you need to separate the birds for whatever reason. You may wish to use the second unit as a recuperation area for sick or injured birds, or the place you accommodate broody hens. You may also find this useful to accommodate the young keets until they mature and can be turned out with the other birds. The secondary unit would not be getting the same level of use as your first unit and so wouldn't carry the same risk of overuse and soil disease.

### Allowing natural light into the coop

You should also ensure that you have several windows in the coop, to let in light during times when the Guineas are locked up. These should preferably be recycled double glazing for obvi-

ous insulating purposes. South facing windows are also ideal as the birds will benefit from most of any daily sunshine. It would also be a good idea to have shutters over these. The effect of this is to screen early morning light. Once the birds realize dawn has broken, they may well start to get restless and wish to get out. In the same way that cockerels crow at the crack of dawn, Guineas are also prone to make a racket.

### Heating the hen house

As mentioned previously, insulation within a cavity wall may cause a condensation build up. However, if you heat the house to an extent, this will keep the atmosphere relatively damp free. During particular cold spells, you may find that an extra heat source is necessary to keep the birds comfortable. This can be a single heat lamp, that will heat the general area to a certain extent, but keep the most needy birds warm, who will readily gravitate to this. For safety reasons, if you do put a heat source into the house, make sure this is clear of any bedding or timber that could possibly cause a fire.

## 10) NESTING/LAYING

### a) Nest building and egg laying

Guinea Fowl are not like chickens as far as nest building and laying eggs. If you build suitable nest boxes, Chickens will find them and happily lay their eggs. Guinea Fowl on the other hand are certainly known to lay their eggs in a purpose built nest box. However, because of instinctively wild tendencies, they more often than not seek to lay their eggs in secluded spots. If the birds are

running free range, they will lay eggs under bushes, or long grass. If contained in a run, they will lay eggs in similar hidden locations given the opportunity.

### b) Nest boxes

Guinea Fowl naturally seek to lay their eggs on the ground in a simple hollow lined with leaves. However, you could also put a few nest boxes above, up to 4ft high (1.2 meters approx), in case the Guineas prefer them. Unlike domestic chicken where nest boxes are usually sited about 2 ft (0.6m) off the floor, Guinea Fowl boxes can be sited at floor level or slightly raised. It is possible to train Guinea Fowl to lay in nest boxes who would otherwise lay on the ground. As soon as you notice a hen on what seems like a ground nest, you can gently pick her up and place her in a nest box. She should soon get the idea and start going into the nest box herself.

Depending on how many Guinea hens you have, you should always site the nest boxes next to each other. The color grey is also said to be attractive to the hens. If you only have several hens, then one or two boxes is probably all that is needed. You don't necessarily have to construct anything for the purpose as there are a number of makeshift options you could use. Some people use pet carriers others have successfully converted tea chests or cardboard boxes. The important thing is that the hen can stand up and turn around, unrestricted.

Nesting boxes can be cubed sections, of as many as you want, although 2 boxes to 6 to 8 hens should be more than enough. The dimensions for these should be approximately 1 to 1.5 ft$^3$ (30.5 cm$^3$ to 46 cm$^3$). You can arrange these in rows and attach to an available wall. These can be simply made out of plywood board, if you cannot buy them cheaply. Remember to leave one end open for the front, and a 4 to 6 inch (10.2 cm 15.2 cm) board at the front to allow easy access and keep the straw bedding for the hens to lay their eggs. You should also attach a landing board or something similar to the perch, for the bird to fly up to and therefore make it easy for them to enter and exit the box.

### c) Where to site nest boxes

You should be aware that if you have a number of Guinea hens they will always prefer to nest together. They are a social, gregarious bird and egg laying is no different. You should therefore place nest boxes literally next to each other. It would also be advisable to site them in as dark an area as possible. You could even encase the nest boxes in some way. Once the nest boxes are in place you could place a barrier around the boxes and leave a 1ft (30cm approx) gap at the front and sides so the birds can walk around. You can then place a hinged lid over the top for you to open up and remove any eggs. The barrier would need an entrance about 8" x 10" (20cm x 25cm approx )for the hens to enter. This would make the inside relatively dark and secluded.

### d) Nests and cleanliness

Any hens that you have, that lay eggs for the purpose of incubating, should be given nesting areas that are as clean as possible. It is best to not have to clean dry feces from the eggs. So any straw or other bedding should always be as clean as possible. This does not mean to say you have to give them fresh bedding every day. But if you notice damp or dirty bedding, particularly the likely nesting areas, then you are advised to change the bedding.

### e) Outside nest covers

If Guinea Fowl are nesting outside on the ground, you should provide suitable ground cover. Use something similar to the tepee/ A frames, outside as nesting areas for the hens to lay eggs. You may also find that they prefer to lay outside and may not even bother with the nest boxes inside the coop.

## 11) GUINEA FOWL EGGS

The following is obviously nothing to do with construction, but is included here as the next logical step to nesting and nest boxes.

### a) Egg laying season

The hens will normally begin laying in spring time, March/April, but this may not start until May if the climate is colder.

Guinea Fowl do not have as great an annual egg yield as chickens. In the wild they would lay perhaps two clutches per year of between 20 and 30 eggs in total. Guinea Fowl that are domesticated lay within a season which usually starts around March and ends September/October. When the hen's are in season they can potentially lay one egg per day. It is not uncommon for a hen to have an annual yield of 180 eggs. However, depending on certain conditions and management, this could be considerably less.

### b) Increasing daylight hours

Unlike chickens who lay eggs throughout the year, Guinea Fowl generally stop egg production in the winter and then start again early spring. As the light is limited in the winter, many egg producers utilize additional artificial light to boost egg production. If you keep chickens with your Guinea Fowl, you could keep an additional light source to boost egg production in the same way.

Some keepers will insist that by extending the light to 14 hours towards fall (autumn), when daylight is less, the Guinea hens will continue laying. Unfortunately this is rarely the case. Guinea Fowl seem to be programmed to a strict season of laying eggs from March to late September/October. You may find one or two continue when others have stopped and start before others in the spring. But they are not the same as Chickens who lay throughout the year and more if you extend the day with artificial lighting.

### c) About Guinea Fowl Eggs

Guinea Fowl eggs have a thicker shell than for example, a chicken egg. The advantage of this is that they tolerate much rougher handling.

Guinea Fowl eggs are smaller in size than a chicken egg at about an average weight of 50 grams (1.8 ounces approx). Chicken eggs by comparison have an average weight of approximately 62 grams (2.2 ounces approx). A turkey egg would have an approximate weight of 85 grams (3 ounces approx). Pheasants have a relatively small size egg with a weight around 30 grams (1.1 ounce approx). Of all the domestic poultry, geese probably have the largest comparable size, around 200 grams (7.1 ounce approx), is not uncommon.

When the young guinea hen first starts to lay, you may notice the eggs are slightly smaller and lighter at first. If you were to weigh the first batches, you may find them weighing approximately 28

grams. By the end of their breeding/egg laying season they should have increased to around 38g to 40g. The eggs will then stay approximately that weight over future seasons.

### Color and shape

As the Guinea Fowl is essentially a wild bird that has been domesticated, it is perhaps no surprise that the egg in shape and color resembles the egg of a game bird. Colors can vary but it is generally assumed to be a shade of brown with occasional speckles.

### Egg construction

The shell itself is largely made up of what is known as the palisade. It is said to make up two thirds of the shell. The soft inner part is known as the mammillary.

### Bloom

The condition or health of the egg can be seen by the appearance. If the egg is healthy it should have a shine to it, and this comes from a fine outer layer known as the cuticle.

### Egg strength

As we know the Guinea Fowl egg has a relatively thick shell in comparison to the domestic chicken egg. Eggs have been tested to establish their breaking strength with the following results. An average chicken egg of approximately 60 grams (2.1 ounces) has a breaking strength of about 4.1 kg (9 pound approx). A Guinea Fowl egg on the other hand of an approximate weight of 40 grams (1.4 ounces) has the breaking strength of around 5 kg (11 pound approx).

### d) Collecting eggs

Whether the guinea eggs are intended for hatching or consumption, you are advised to collect these on a daily basis. If the eggs are for consumption, you do not need to do any more than collect them and either refrigerate them or store them in a cool place. If you can get hold of egg trays then so much the better. If you buy eggs from the supermarket, you may also wish to keep the egg cartons for future use. Failing all of that, a suitable container, that you may wish to line with sawdust or some cloth material will suffice.

The ideal storage temperature for eggs is said to be about 12.8° C to 15.6° C (55° F to 60° F).

### When is the best time to collect eggs?

Guinea Fowl have a tendency to lay eggs around noon. So if you are collecting the eggs on a daily basis, do this either mid afternoon, evening or first thing the next day.

### Collecting eggs and leaving pot/ dummy eggs

You may hear that leaving a pot egg is desirable when you collect eggs from a nest. This is a good idea whilst the hen is laying and to not upset her so she abandons the nest. But eventually the hen will go broody as she believes she has a clutch of eggs that need incubating. There is probably not a lot you can do about this, as the important thing is to encourage her to continue laying. Once she does go broody, it is best to remove anything from the nest. She will probably abandon the nest and continue laying once she has stopped being broody.

### Is it safe to eat fertilized eggs?

If you intend to eat your Guinea Fowl eggs, then you need not worry about whether you are eating fertilized eggs or not. When chickens or Guinea Fowl are kept with their male counterpart, the male will automatically mate with the female. However not all eggs will necessarily be fertilized, which depends on a number of factors. Eggs that are fertilized and are left with a broody hen, who begins to incubate, are likely to develop and eventually hatch out. This is why you need to collect eggs each day and store them at a low temperature, preferably refrigerated. Fertilized eggs have the potential to develop into embryos, but only if they are heated at an optimum temperature. Un-heated eggs will remain dormant and are perfectly alright for consumption.

# Chapter Six

# Guinea Fowl Feeding; Feeders and Drinkers

Once you have taken care of accommodation needs, you will have to equip the coop with drinkers and feeders. These can be as elaborate or simple as you want. There is nothing to stop you using shallow buckets or trays as food or water dispensers. However, the following offers advice on what you will need. We will then cover all aspects of feeding your Guinea Fowl.

## 1) FEEDERS AND DRINKERS

### a) How many feeders and drinkers do you need?

If you are wondering how many feeders and drinkers you should have for the birds you have. The birds are unlikely to all need to feed or drink at the same time. If you had for example 10 to 20 birds, then there is no harm in starting with 1 decent sized feed hopper and the same for a drinker. If you expand or have more birds to start with then increase appropriately.

### b) Choosing drinkers and feeders

When you are considering buying drinkers and feeders, always be aware that you should be buying specific feeders and drinkers for the keets. There are specialist types specifically for chicks or keets that are smaller than the type used for adults. You are strongly advised to buy those types of dispensers. This is particularly important for the drinker as you do not want to risk the keets getting wet and chilled or much worse, drowning. The specific feeders are highly recommended. But you will hear of some keepers who spread the chick crumbs/turkey starter on a large shallow dish. The only problem with this is that you will get droppings from the keets that will contaminate the feed.

Once the birds are adult, then you can improvise and use makeshift feeders and drinkers, without worrying about the same risks.

### c) Which feeders are best?

The type of feeders that have segmented sections so the birds cannot literally get into the trough, often work out best. They generally restrict head movement, although it doesn't stop the birds from picking feed out and dropping it on the floor. Any food that does end up on the floor can be left for a day but should be cleaned up sometime the next day. You do not want the keets in particular to be eating food that is either contaminated with feces or becomes damp, stale and moldy.

However, for adult birds, ideally you also want to avoid any possible contamination or wastage. So for dry food pellet or mash, use some sort of hopper dispenser. These can be either cylinder hoppers that you hang from a beam or free standing that you would attach to a wall or sit on a block platform.

Also as mentioned hanging feeders offer a good all round food dispenser. Provided that they are hung from a beam at a height that all birds can easily get at the food, they should remain free from any dirt. They are also useful as the birds are unable to scratch in the food tray. Unfortunately it is not always easy to prevent the birds flicking or dropping food out as they eat. Hopefully they shouldn't waste too much food and any that does fall on the floor should eventually be picked up by the birds. If the wastage seems a lot, a possible solution is to raise the height. Again you should ensure that all the birds can feed from it.

**TIP:** If you store dry food in an outbuilding, this should ideally be kept in an airtight container. Even if you leave bags of feed in a locked up shed undercover, there is still a risk that you will encourage mice and rats.

## 2) DRINKERS

### a) Which drinkers are best?

I would recommend that you use tough plastic water drinkers in preference to metal. Some cheap metal drinkers can corrode over time. You also need to be careful not to be tempted by cheap plastic containers either. This is false economy as they can deteriorate if exposed to extreme temperatures, hot or cold.

### Water dispenser

Water can be dispensed in a similar way to feed hoppers, except they are generally not hung, but rather sat on a raised block. You simply fill the main hopper and a small opening in the base allows so much to flow into a reservoir dish. The birds then take this as they need it and the dish replenishes itself automatically.

**TIP:** Be sure to check the dispensers on a daily basis, and certainly clean the water container out regularly, to avoid slime and bacteria build up.

### Nipple drinkers

Nipple drinkers are efficient and easier to manage than regular drinkers. However, many keepers suggest that the birds benefit more so, from the regular drinkers that allow the birds to dip their beaks, and washing them each time. The disadvantage with nipple drinkers is that they need plumbing to either a mains water supply or storage tank. They also need fixing which therefore means re-siting them is not as easy as a portable drinker.

### Alternative water dispenser

You may also find that once your Guinea Fowl are adults, then you can use other water containers. Some people use large shallow bowls, but never attempt to use anything like this for young keets as there is a high risk of them drowning.

### b) Cleaning the water dispenser

Whatever the water system, this can soon become contaminated if not regularly cleaned. Food particles and other contaminants picked up on the birds beak, can soon lead to a build up of bacteria.

Do not forget that you should regularly clean any water containers to prevent bacteria growth. It is unlikely you will need to do this more than once per week for a quick clean and a scrub with a brush or similar. Then around once a month, give it a thorough disinfect/ sterilize to keep on top of any bacteria growth. You may find that you have to do it more often than that or you can leave it for longer. You will soon be able to judge this for yourself depending on usage and if the weather is hot. The quick weekly clean can be done where the drinkers are located, unless they are inside the hen house, which you should take outside so as not to get the litter wet. The sterilization is best done away from the enclosure so that the Guinea Fowl are not in contact with any chemical residue.

If you have to clean the water receptacles, a cheap solution can be made with bleach. Thick bleach is obviously more concentrated. You can make a solution with about ½ a cup/mug (150ml ¼ of a pint) in approximately 53 US pints (44 UK pints) (25 litres) of water. If you either spray or submerge equipment with this diluted mixture and leave for

15 to 20 minutes, it should kill bacteria and sterilize the equipment. You will of course need to thoroughly rinse this. You certainly do not want the birds ingesting any of this solution or any other disinfectant. Chlorine has always been known as a cheap and effective sterilizer. However some bacteria in some countries is resistant to chlorine, therefore it may be necessary in some cases to use a different type of disinfectant.

## c) Siting drinkers

The recommended height if a **suspended or bell drinker** is said to be so that as the bird stands in its normal position, the top of the birds back should roughly be in line with the bottom of the drinker.

**Nipple drinkers,** are usually best positioned at a height that the bird is reaching upward for. If you decided to incorporate nipple drinkers then as a guide you would need 1 drinker for approximately every 10 birds. The advantages of nipple drinkers is less wastage, less contamination, and it is not necessary to regularly clean the unit. You do however have to ensure they are running efficiently making sure the birds are getting sufficient water. If you have birds at different ages and therefore height variations, then it will be necessary to be able to adjust the heights in some way or have a number of drinkers staggered at different heights. As mentioned the height should make the bird reach up and certainly not stoop. The other key point to take note of, is that the feet of the bird needs to remain on the ground. If the birds seem to be stretching on their tip toes, the drinker is too high.

## d) Supplying water

Be aware that both during hot summers and cold winters, regular water supply is a must. They will be particularly thirsty in the summer, so it is best to provide an alternative supply outside, that is filled on a daily basis. Also in the summer there is a greater occurrence of bacteria and disease growth. So cleaning any water receptacles on a daily basis is advised.

## A fresh clean water supply

As previously mentioned, clean fresh water should be provided on a daily basis, at least inside the enclosure. A good sized water dispenser should hold 3 to 4 gallons (11.4 litre to 15 litre approx) of water. Again, remove any straw or dirt that may have dropped or been flicked into the drinking part. You may wish to stand the drinker on some platform, so that it is kept off the ground. Make sure this isn't too high and that all the birds can reach inside to take a drink comfortably. You could also create a platform perhaps using ply board that is wide enough for the drinker and for the birds to jump on. You may also decide to create something similar to the wire covered dropping pit for the ladder perch. You will probably have to clean the pit out from time to time as it can sometimes retain a lot of damp bedding below the drinker.

## How much water will they drink?

For adult Guinea Fowl assume as a rough guide that 30 birds will drink approximately 3 US gallons (11 litres approx). 2 UK gallons approx is = (11 litres approx), of water. These figures are on a daily basis, during warm/hot sum-

mer months. Obviously in the winter time, this will be quite a bit less. So as a rough guide to how big your water containers or container should be assume those amounts.

### How much does water weigh?

You should also be aware that 1 US gallon of water weighs 3.8 kg approx or 8 pound 6 ounces.

1 UK gallon = 4.5kg. So a 3 to 5 gallon drinker, will be heavy to say the least particularly if you have to carry that or several to the Guinea Fowl enclosure. Of course you will not need to carry water if you have a long hose pipe to fill the drinkers, or perhaps drinkers fed from a water tank. Automatic watering systems are excellent, but may be a problem with freezing in the winter.

### Problems with water freezing

During particularly harsh cold winters the water dispensers, whether free standing or pipe fed, can freeze. For pipes it may be necessary to lag the pipes in much the same way as domestic house plumbing. Water fountains may need a temporary heating pad that the fountain sits on. Always follow manufacturer instructions and recommendations when using any electrical heating appliance.

Also during the winter, whether the birds free range or not, are likely to need supplementary vegetation. This is important for them as it is vital for effective digestion. There are many options available including vegetable leaves that you have left over. It may also be a good idea to contact a friendly greengrocer. They would no doubt be only too pleased for you to take away waste leaves and such like, that they would be paying someone to dispose of. Alfalfa bales are popular, and we will talk more about that later.

### Freeze proof waterer

If water freezing becomes a problems for you I would advise you to research 'freeze proof poultry waterer's'. Either do a Google search for 'freeze proof poultry waterer', where you will find some excellent articles. You could also look at a number of You-tube videos that will give you further ideas on this approach.

## 3) FEEDING

ever, it is important to be aware that a good blended formula, such as pellets or crumbs, are extremely important to the health of the growing keet, and indeed, adult bird. Deficiencies in a diet can occur at any age. In the same way that we will take vitamin and mineral tablets, you should view supplementary feed likewise. Many diseases and disorders can be prevented by ensuring your birds are receiving as much nutrients as they need. This is particularly important at the growth stages for keets. But it is also important at the reproductive stage as the birds need to be at peak fitness. During the spring/ summer months, the

### A) GENERAL FEED INFORMATION

There is no need to develop complex scientific knowledge regarding the exact nutrients that Guinea Fowl need at different stages of development. How-

birds should be able to find extra natural supplementary feed. But as vegetation and insects diminish and die off, with the onset of winter, then even adult birds will suffer if they do not receive sufficient nutrients.

Guinea Fowl, much like any other animal, require a basic diet that consists of protein, carbohydrate, fat and water. Water can be a source of disease so water dispensers must be regularly cleaned. You may have an automatic water system and possibly find that diseases eventually develop despite you cleaning the receptacle on a regular basis. In such cases a build up bacteria in the pipe work or from joints could be a cause. In which case it may be necessary to treat this with a suitable sterilizer and flush the whole system clean. If your birds are largely free range and perhaps have access to a stream or river, you may find you do not have any such problem. However they must be kept away from any contaminated water source such as stagnating water. It is surprising how few diseases, free range birds exhibit in comparison to birds that are largely housed.

## B) THE DIGESTIVE SYSTEM AND PROCESS

Food is generally stored in the crop, but this depends on whether the bird is particularly hungry, and if so it is likely to pass through to the gizzard. If the bird is not in immediate need for food the crop will store this for quite a number of hours until needed. The crop also has a large capacity of storage, which is useful as the bird can pick up food that it does not necessarily need, but does not wish to leave behind. Guinea Fowl are said to process food in the space of a few hours.

Under normal circumstances, i.e. the bird is not immediately hungry, the food will pass from the crop to the proventriclus, or stomach. Hydrochloric acid juices and pepsin are released and digestion of food begins. The food then passes to the gizzard, which is a hard muscular organ, that works by an opposing contracting motion. Along with grit, the food is effectively ground to a paste. The food finally passes to the intestine were it is absorbed by the body.

## C) FOOD SOURCES

There are a number of food sources that you should be aware of as a keeper of Guinea Fowl. The following offers an overview of the most commonly used feed types.

### Protein

Pellets for adults or crumbs for growing keets is an obvious source of controlled protein as well as carbohydrates and other essential elements. Do not forget that adult birds, will get a good percentage of protein and carbohydrates from cracked corn, wheat and other grains and seeds. Wheat is said to contain approximately 10 % of protein. You can also feed beans such as soya but they may prove to be expensive.

### Insect protein

Among other essential ingredients, insects provide a good source of protein for Guinea Fowl as well as all other birds. The following National Geographic article

*http://news.na-tionalgeographic.com/news/2013/13/130514-edible-insects-entomophagy-science-food-bugs-beetles/*

gives an example of 100 grams of red ants consisting of 14 grams of protein. As well as insects, protein can be found in worms and many available grubs. Other sources of insect protein are as follows: Tics, grasshoppers, ants, centipedes, beetles, locust, flies, spiders, cockroaches, snails, moths, termites, caterpillars among many others. As you will no doubt be aware, a lot of these are found in and around most households and some are obvious pests.

### Protein content for adults

Protein content for adults is important and they should at least have access to feed that has a protein content of 15 or 16% minimum. This is very important during fall (autumn) and through winter. Once the natural sources of protein such as insects etc die off, they have no way of providing the protein for themselves. Some keepers will even advocate giving their birds an even higher protein percentage depending on extreme winter temperatures.

### Vegetation

Poultry need vegetation for digestion and is vital for their health and wellbeing. You can often see a poorly looking bird perk up when fed chopped up leaves. Clover, grass and chickweed are recommended but most vegetable leaves are suitable. Charcoal is also considered to be another excellent digestive aid.

### Pellets or mash

Mash, is basically ground up feed in a rough powder form. Some keepers and breeders prefer this as it is easy for the birds to eat. The drawbacks are that because it is dusty, it can cause breathing problems. It is also potentially wasteful. If it gets flicked out of a feed hopper and end up on the floor, it may not get picked up by birds scratching about later. There is also the risk that it

could get mixed up with contaminated litter/bedding etc, on the floor and cause some sort of disease. Pellets on the other hand are a less problematic alternative.

### Grain

If you decide to purchase corn, wheat or other grains, you should certainly shop around. It can prove to be expensive, so bear in mind the cost factor. For convenience it may be tempting to purchase grain from your local pellet/crumb supplier. This is all well and good if they are competitively priced.

It may be a better option to contact farmers in your area to find out if they would be happy supply you. As they grow it themselves you are effectively cutting out the middle man, and therefore they are bound to sell it cheaper as a result.

Whatever is available in your area you should check the protein and carbohydrate content. A quick Internet search will reveal typical Percentage values per 100g, such as the ones that follow

| SOURCE | PROTEIN | CARBOHYDRATE | FAT |
|--------|---------|--------------|-----|
| MAIZE/CORN | 9.4 | 74 | 4.7 |
| RICE | 7.1 | 80 | 0.7 |
| WHEAT | 12.6 | 71 | 1.5 |
| SOYBEAN | 13 | 11 | 6.8 |

Source: *http://en.wikipedia.org/wiki/Wheat*

### Feeding grains

Cereals are said to make up most of the Guinea Fowl diet and this can be up to 80%. These can be fed whole or cracked corn, but they actually prefer this ground to an extent but not too fine.

Small amounts of grain should be fed whole. This is especially beneficial if harmful bacteria is present in the intestine. Whole grains promote extra acidity which kill the harmful bacteria. Fish or bone meal is also an excellent dietary addition.

### Corn/maize

Maize/corn: contains 65% carbohydrate, but is quite low in vitamins and minerals. Relatively low in protein at only about 7% to 9%. It is often fed as a bulk ingredient of up to 70% of a diet.

### Wheat

Wheat usually contains about 9% to 12% protein, however this depends on the strain. It is quite high in vitamins and minerals. Many birds will tend to favor wheat as opposed to other grains. It is also therefore considered a useful main dietary ingredient. Some people suggesting this should constitute about 60% of the diet.

### Barley

Barley is not as popular as wheat as the protein and carbohydrate levels are lower in comparison. So although this is considered a good addition to a diet it is only likely to consist of no more than 50% of the diet.

### Oats

Oats are high in fibre, but lower in value compared to the others, and therefore should not really make more than 20% of an overall diet.

## 4) SUPPLEMENTARY FEEDING

### a) How much feed to buy?

How much feed you initially should buy is difficult to say, as this depends on how many keets you raise, or Guinea Fowl you buy as adult birds. Most suppliers supply them in bags of 20 kg anyway, so it is unlikely the average keeper will run out after a day. But certainly monitor how much they feed, then you can easily work out how soon you need to order should you be running low. We will look at what your birds are likely to eat per week, so do not worry too much about this now.

### b) Where to feed the birds

You should always feed the birds indoors, and certainly not leave feed outside, as this will only attract vermin. Providing the coop is vermin proof, you can feed them liberally. Otherwise restrict the amount of feed to how much you know they generally eat in a day.

### c) Filling the feed hoppers

Having said that, although these dispensers can hold approximately 20 kg (44 pounds) of food I would advise you only fill this up as much as the birds are eating every couple of days or so. If there is a damp issue, the food can quickly spoil and become stale. There is also a possibility that mice or rats could be encouraged into the hen house by the regular supply of food.

Foraging free range and supplementing the feed

Some people prefer to have a feed hopper available for them all of the time. This is a good idea providing the birds are only taking what they need to supplement free range foraging. Guinea Fowl do have a tendency to eat little and often. Therefore many keepers recommend providing supplementary food on an ad-lib basis. If you find that your Guinea Fowl do not seem as keen as you had hoped, to clean up the insect pest problems, then you may need to control the supplementary feed.

If your guineas are running free range during the summer, then they will forage for a lot of insects, seeds and vegetation. However they will be encouraged more so if you restrict any supplementary feed you give them. If during the spring and summer months you continue liberally feeding them pellets or corn etc, then they will be less keen to forage for insects pests etc.

### d) Problems with ad-lib feeding

If however they seem to be filling up on the ad-lib feed you give them and not really bothering ridding your property of insect pests, then try the following. What you need to do is give them small amounts of corn or pellets at sporadic, unpredictable times, as you are giving them a treat. If the Guinea Fowl know that at approximately 8 am for example, every morning, they get this feed, they will wait for it and waste foraging opportunities.

So in summary, during the spring to late summer season, when vegetation and insects are plentiful, Guinea Fowl will forage for most of their intake needs. You should only therefore need to give them a feed in the morning and a feed in the evening. You may have a particular insect pest or weed problem that you wish the Guinea Fowl to deal with. What you ideally want is for the Guinea Fowl to eradicate this problem which they are very good at doing.

### e) Free range foraging

Large parcels of land, rough, scrub or some wooded area, that is not used for anything in particular, are excellent foraging grounds for a flock of Guinea Fowl. They will make full use of clearing insect pests and keeping down certain vegetation. Ideally you want them to feed on the natural food source available. You certainly do not want the birds to eat whatever you give them and have none or little interest in going in search of anything extra. Some people find that their birds will have unlimited feed available to them and still want to go in search of insects and green stuff etc.

If your Guinea Fowl are completely free range from March to late September and you live in a location that has abundant natural resources, assume that they are foraging on a lot of nutritional food stuff. If however they are confined to an outdoor enclosure that may have vegetation growing and insects in the area, they are unlikely to be getting anywhere near the same amount of nutrition. You therefore will need to provide more commercial feed and green food.

### f) Supplementary feed when the birds are not free ranging

For keets finely chopped or grated carrot root and leaves are a very good supplementary food. Swedes and turnips are also useful given whole for adult birds to pick at.

You can also feed lucerne, alfalfa, kale, cabbage, peas, lentils and beans. However, beans need to be soaked and minced. Other sources include: Palm kernels, most seeds, berries and apples.

### Feeding eggs as a protein source

Some keepers recommend feeding eggs as a protein or calcium supplement. If you consider this, it is probably best to disguise the egg in some way. It is probably best cooked and mixed with something to disguise it. You certainly do not want your Guinea Fowl to see eggs as a food source and start raiding nests and eating the eggs.

### Alternative feed

Screenings are something you should definitely inquire about if you have a local feed mill you can easily commute to. You may have to take a bulk load of this, but quality screenings are an excellent source of cheap protein feed. There are all manner of screenings from just about every seed or grain you can think of. These include corn, wheat, oat, grass seed, pea, barley, lentil etc. They can also be the dust from the processing.

Most have a crude protein content of 10 to 17%. Some are quite low such as oats at 4 to 8% and buckwheat at around 4%.

Screenings are basically the waste or by-product from the main product that a mill will produce. Seeds pass through screens that effectively clean the seed or strip it of hulls, chaff, weed seeds etc.

### Supplementary feed garlic and onion

A natural food source and medicine that is considered very beneficial to both keets and adults is garlic and onion. A clove of garlic placed in a water dispenser for the keets will act as an excellent tonic. They will equally benefit the keets and adults from a health point of view. Common diseases that seem to afflict Guinea Fowl are coccidiosis, worms and respiratory diseases. In adults, garlic and onion have proved to be natural remedies for colds, flu and other conditions. In this same manner, they will also protect and act as a preventative aid for poultry.

As a food additive, one clove can be chopped or minced and mixed with the daily amount of food. One clove should be enough for 3 adult birds or 6 keets.

### Supplementary feed; apples

Cooking and crab apples are an excellent food source and tonic for poultry in general. Guinea Fowl will avidly devour these given the opportunity. Apple cider vinegar is also said to be highly beneficial to both keets and adult birds. Apple cider vinegar has been used for centuries as a natural remedy for humans suffering certain ailments. It is known to alleviate cold symptoms, fight diabetes, cancer, heart problems and high cholesterol among others. For poultry it can act as a natural anti-biotic. It can therefore act as a preventative medication for infectious bacteria and diseases. In addition, it can go a large way to boosting the immune system, among other uses. You can buy this cheaply from many pet suppliers and should follow carefully the instructions for use.

### Supplementary feed: Natural weeds and plants

Many naturally growing weeds and plants are excellent sources of vegetation for Guinea Fowl, and these include:
Water and land cress, fennel, clover, dandelion (the whole plant), chickweed, thistle, wild fruits such as blackberry, cleavers etc. Nettles which grow naturally in the wild are also excellent. It has always been considered to have many benefits as a natural medicine. Gardeners will know the potency of nettle as a natural fertilizer.

Washed and dried seaweed is also something worth investigating. Obviously this will be of great benefit to you if you live on or near the coast and can obtain a regular supply. Depending on the type e.g. kelp, wakame, green laver etc, they are rich in protein, around 25%, carbohydrate 40 to 50%. They are also rich in many vitamins and minerals such as B1 and B12, iron, sodium, calcium, potassium etc. Because of the richness, they only need to be given up to about 5% of the birds diet. It may be best if you obtain this from your supplier to start with until you establish how best to feed this. If you can get this locally, find out which type it is and whether or not you have to cook it or whether you can feed it raw.

The other, non seaweed vegetation mentioned, only needs to be picked and given to the birds as it is, or unless they can forage this for themselves.

## 5) WINTER FEEDING.

As we have already seen, in the winter, most natural food sources will disappear and it will be necessary to provide extra, supplementary food. Supplementary feeds you can try during winter include mixed bird seed, fat balls or suet blocks.

### a) Winter vegetation

Alfalfa (Lucerne) bales are probably the best winter vegetation substitute feed for Guinea Fowl. Depending on what is available at the time, 3rd cutting is said to be the best as this offers more leaves. You generally find that the Guinea Fowl do not eat all of the alfalfa, usually leaving the stalks.

You can of course use bean sprouts, lettuce, spinach but avoid vegetation that is overly fibrous or stringy as this can cause problem such as impacted crops.

### b) Alfalfa bales

If you can stock up on alfalfa bales you will have all the green vegetation alternative that you need. If not then most vegetable leaves that are available throughout the year, including lettuce, cabbage, kale etc, will be suitable. A bale of alfalfa will weigh about 90 pounds (40 kg approx). 30 birds can get through about 8 or these bales and should last 4 or 5 months during winter.

The following are a few US and UK suppliers:

Please note this is not an exhaustive list. Nor are they necessarily recommendations or an indication of the cheapest. They are certainly a good place to start, and as with any product you buy, you should always shop around. You are recommended to buy bales and buy in bulk if you can. Also in the first instance, try and find a local farm that supplies alfalfa. You will no doubt find more by searching Google for your area.

### c) Alfalfa suppliers USA:

**Hay Country:** This is an excellent resource that lists about 50 pages of suppliers.
*https://www.haycountry.com/alfalfa-hay-for-sale/*

**Internet Hay Exchange:** Another excellent resource as above.
*http://www.hayexchange.com/ca.php*

There are many more local resources that you can easily find by doing a quick search on Google for 'alfalfa hay for sale USA', or a similar search term for your area.

### d) Alfalfa suppliers UK

Old Manor Farm: *http://www.oldmanorfarm. com/hay.asp*

**Valley View Animal Feeds:** *http://www.valleyviewanimal- feeds.com/ourcornishalfalfa.htm*

**Hay Net:** *http://www.hay-net.com/ alfalfa.htm*

**British Association of Green Crop Driers:** *http://www.bagcd.org/pro- ducers/*

## 6) NECESSARY FOOD FOR EGG LAYING BIRDS

### *How much protein do egg laying hens need?*

Hens have been known to have a higher egg production, when fed on 14% protein, than hens fed on a higher protein content up to 18%.

In order to produce quality eggs, the hen herself has to be healthy and relatively free from disease. Defective eggs can be a good indication that the hen is defective in some way. It could also be that her diet and environment is not as good as it needs to be.

Birds that are on free range are likely to seek nutrition and elements that their body is telling them they need. In most cases free range hens remain fit and healthy and produce the best eggs. It will therefore come as no surprise that if the hens cannot access this naturally, such as those living in an enclosed avi- ary, then we as keepers must provide

these elements.

Corn and layers pellets are also recommended. The layers feed is par- ticularly beneficial as there is still a high level of protein. As the name suggests layers feed is usually given to hens during their laying season. The extra protein is needed for egg production. The protein content is usually around 18%, although some can be quite a bit less.

## 7) OTHER CONSIDERATIONS WHEN FEEDING GUINEA FOWL

### *a) Storing food*

Do you have sound and secure storage areas for storing food, and other items connected with the birds up keep? If you are on a small holding, you no doubt have existing buildings for such purposes. If however you intend to use a reasonable sized garden, then space may be limited. In all cases it would be beneficial to have spare space in case you decide to expand your operation. If nothing else, I would recommend you store food likely to attract rodents, in your house.

### *b) Protecting the food from vermin, moisture etc*

Any feed that you have should be protected from vermin. If you have bales of hay, straw or alfalfa, this may not be easy. But any bags of expensive feed you buy should be placed in air tight containers, usually plastic. This will keep them as fresh as possible for as long as possible but also deter rodents that will add to your food bill. You should also store them away from anything likely to affect the feed such as heat, moisture and direct sunlight. When you buy feed always check the date of manufacture or use by or best before date. You need to be buying the freshest feed and certainly do not want to pay full price for something that is going or has gone out of date.

### c) Avoid feeding Guinea Fowl certain foods

Be careful of feeding your Guinea Fowl anything that may cause unwanted problems. As well as eggs, some people will feed them vegetables that they grow. Others will feed scraps of bread. This is all well and good if you do not mind them destroying your vegetable patches etc. But if you have neighbors and the birds are on free range, any such items your neighbors have laying around will also fall victim to the Guinea Fowl and be quickly devoured. Fair enough if your neighbors do not mind. But if the birds become destructive or a nuisance then you are asking for trouble.

Encouraging Guinea Fowl to feed on anything will only encourage them to search the things they particularly like. So feeding leaves and left over vegetables could pose problems if you grow your own. Or worse still, if your neighbor grows their own. The last thing you want it to find your guineas have invaded a neighbors veg patch and destroyed their prized tomatoes or kale leaf. It can happen so again beware and exercise caution if in doubt.

### d) Scavenging

You have probably seen wild birds flock to your bird table if you have one. Wild birds probably have unlimited choice to naturally growing seeds and berries etc. However, they will always seek food that is easiest to gather, and therefore seek food from your bird table first. Guinea Fowl and other poultry are no different, and will no doubt seek any available free food locally. Unfortunately this could also include them trespassing onto your neighbors property for food that they leave out.

### e) Feeding: An important fact about mixing chickens with Guinea Fowl

Guinea Fowl keets in particular need a greater protein intake than baby chicks. Be aware however, that high levels of protein produce an excess uric acid build up, that can be harmful to any animal. This can cause problems in bodily organs such as the kidneys. It is also known to affect the joints and in birds such as chickens can cause gout.

It is therefore important that when mixing the birds, e.g. baby chickens and Guinea Fowl, that a lower protein feed is used for the adults. For this reason, it may be best to feed the birds separately, or at least until the keets are no longer in need of the extra protein.

Interestingly breeders/meat producers, have also noticed that giving young birds extra food to increase muscle yield, shows negligible increases of 1 or 2%. The food is expensive and in these cases has proved unnecessary and costly. Any additional protein or carbohydrate usually shows weight gain as fat deposits.

### Cod liver oil

Many keepers of poultry insist on dosing birds with cod liver oil, particularly in the winter and of course when the bird is ill. It has many health benefits and is well worth adding to their daily diet.

## 8) FEEDING GRIT

### *a) Have a ready supply of grit*

Another vital ingredient to the Guinea Fowl diet is grit, ideally in the form of oyster shell. Once again they should have a constant supply of this which is vital for their digestive process as well as for egg shell production. Nothing particularly elaborate is needed for a grit dispenser; a shallow bucket is suitable. But if you wish, you can buy a hopper type dispenser, or make a simple wooden box dispenser. The important thing is to place it at a height off the floor, that will allow easy access for the birds. You can follow the same height that we talked about for siting a feed hopper. Although any that is thrown out of the container isn't wasted as such, as it is not perishable and will likely be picked up when they scratch about the floor.

Grit serves two purposes. Firstly dissolved calcium is essential for egg shell production. Occasionally you may have come across what appears to be an egg without the shell. The likely reason for this is that the hen has not had access to enough grit. Oyster shells are preferable as they easily dissolve and are especially high in carbonate of lime. Other types of grit do not dissolve as quickly, but provide the same function.

The second function of grit is to aid the gizzard. As partially digested food passes through into the gizzard, the muscular action of the gizzard along with the grit effectively grinds and processes the food.

Wild birds naturally have vast sources of gravel and grit to choose from. Birds within an enclosure do not have that luxury. In the same way that you need to ensure the birds receive a balanced diet and green food, grit must also be provided.

You should also be aware that the size of the grit is important depending on the bird and the stage of its development. For example feeding keets chick or turkey crumbs will not require grit as part of the digestive process. In fact the gizzard will function and process food without grit or at least limited access to it. But it functions far better with as much grit as the bird needs. However, you do not have the same choice with egg production for obvious reasons. As soon as you start to feed keets any type of grain or seed then please bear in mind, they will require grit. In this respect it would be preferable if you have an appropriate size of grit for them to easily swallow about one to several mm in size, depending on the age. You can buy special graded grit for keets. You will also find that many keepers advocate using sand for younger keets.

## b) Grit dispenser

For the purposes of a grit dispenser a lot of people tend to recommend rabbit feeders. The main function of these is that they are hopper fed, and they have an easy access trough.

As previously mentioned, you will probably find some grit ending up on the floor. Unless you see a potential problem with the grit getting contaminated with feces, the birds will eventually pick this up.

Among the many types of grit you can buy, you may find that having an extra dispenser with sand or even a sand pit or throwing this on the ground, will offer a good alternative. I would however recommend giving them a supply of grit, oyster shell or otherwise. Also do not be too surprised if the birds do not seem to eat a lot of grit. They will eat as much as they need and may well be getting a supply on free range or in your outside enclosure. Sand is often good to mix with a dry soil patch. This will serve as a dust bath but again allow the birds the option to pick among it for a grit substitute if they need it.

# CHAPTER SEVEN

# BREEDING: INITIAL STAGES

We will cover the next two chapters on breeding, in two parts. This first part will give you an introduction to the information you will need to know, such as breeding stock, incubators and what to expect when hatching eggs.

# 1) Breeding Guinea Fowl

## a) Check list for breeding success

» In general for the best breeding and hatching success the following should be observed.

» Fit and healthy hens and cocks

» Nutritious quality feed, supplemented with sufficient vegetation and grit.

» A recommended protein requirement for breeding purpose of 13.5% to 14.5%

» Cocks that are not expected to service too many hens

» Eggs that are collected daily, carefully stored and labeled, and kept at an optimum temperature that is neither too warm or too cold.

» Eggs kept that are as clean as possible.

» Also during this period, the birds will need as much fresh air, freedom and exercise as possible to develop fitness levels.

There is no doubt that for optimum results, the birds need enough protein and other nutrients. However, some would argue whether you need to feed either layers or breeders pellets. It all depends what access they have to natural food sources, free range for example. It will certainly do no harm to offer these supplement feeds, but with experience you may find that the birds manage as well on lower quality, cheaper feeds as well as free range protein.

Also remember that excessive consumption of protein can lead to uric acid build up, that admittedly is more detrimental to Chickens, but will certainly have an adverse effect on Guinea Fowl. This is especially problematic if you are running a mixed flock of Guinea Fowl with Chickens.

### *Achieving Breeding Success*

**Protein requirements**

Feeding corn and other grains through the winter season is certainly an excellent way to provide protein and carbohydrates, necessary to sustain them. But during the egg laying and breeding season, you are advised to feed layers or breeders pellets. These compounds are reasonably high in protein and can contain up to 20%.

The pellets are a formulated compound that should ensure the hens receive all the necessary nutrients, that the hens in particular will need for egg production.

## b) Facts About Breeding Guinea Fowl?

Mature hens between 1 and 2 years of age are arguably said to be at their best. Again, birds at that age may produce stronger keets than a much older bird. But there is nothing to say hens of over 2 years plus, will be less successful.

Obviously relatively older hens will no doubt get to a point where they are less effective than younger hens. And in the same way, you can assume that older cock birds will be less virile and potent.

## What age should the male Guinea begin breeding?

The male Guinea Fowl or cock, reaches a satisfactory sexual maturity after 6 months of age. By this age they should be able to produce satisfactory levels of semen in order to successfully fertilize eggs. The female is usually at point of lay, that is able to produce eggs and therefore reproduce, by 28 weeks of age.

It is debatable as to optimum breeding ages for the cock and the hen. In some cases a cockerel of less than a year old is considered to be more potent and virile. This could well be the case, but does not necessarily mean that older cock birds are any less potent or virile.

## Breeding stock

Your breeding stock in general should be healthy and vital. Breeders will always endeavor to keep the best birds possible and remove less able or vital birds. If you keep Guinea Fowl as pets, you will no doubt wish to keep all the birds you have, and keep them as happy and healthy as possible. However, for optimum breeding purposes you are advised to only breed from the best specimens you have. This means that any birds you have that have obvious weaknesses or defects, can be loved as pets, but may not be the best birds to breed from.

## How long are Guinea Fowl productive for?

A hens egg producing capacity and therefore reproduction, is active for 5 years or more. The male semen production seems to decline after 3 years.

Guinea Fowl pairing up for mating Guinea Fowl hens are known to be monogamous and will mate with the same partner for life. The male on the other hand are known to mate with several hens. Whether this is through necessity, if for example there is only one male to several hens, or by choice is debatable.

## Cock to hen ratio

If you are managing a flock however, you should ensure that there is at least one cock Guinea Fowl for every 5 or 6 female. Particularly if you intend to breed from your Guinea Fowl, you do not want to over work any cock birds you have. The likelihood is that he will not be as potent as he could be. When the services of the male is diluted as it were, you may find that hen eggs are infertile or the offspring is not as virile as they could be.

## The mating ritual

Around the time that the Guinea Fowl begin the reproduction process, you may notice the birds behaving strangely. During mating season, you will no doubt notice the Guinea Fowl mating ritual. Both sexes are known to perform a darting, courtship dance to entice a prospective mate.

## Male aggression during mating season

Guinea Fowl cock birds, much the same as other male species, will often fight with other male birds for the right to mate with a female. You should not therefore be surprised if you encounter two males fighting or one chasing the other. During breeding season male Guinea Fowl will become more aggressive and territorial. In enclosed areas

therefore it may not be wise to have too many cocks running together. Even in free range situations, cocks will invariably chase and fight each other.

### *What color will your new keets be?*

If you are breeding from a pair of Guinea Fowl and both parents are for example white, do not be surprised if some of the keets are a different color. Many breeders find that because of a diverse genetic history, that the male or female may produce keets of any color from a shade of blue to any shade of brown.

## 2) HATCHING FERTILE EGGS WITH AN INCUBATOR

You may decide at some point to hatch some fertilized eggs in an incubator. Incubating and hatching eggs can offer a fascinating aspect to this hobby. The equipment can also be purchased relatively cheaply if you shop around. Check available information on the Internet and once you begin to get familiar with what is available and your own requirements, you can shop around on sites such as ebay.

**NOTE:** If using an incubator, always follow manufacturer instructions. The temperature and humidity requirements will remain the same, but the specifics of the incubators may vary.

### a) Using a small incubator to hatch eggs

Still air incubators should be suitable for a beginner. A quick search on ebay should reveal many reasonably priced incubators with a capacity that start at 10 or 12 eggs.

### b) Are incubators a cheaper option to buying day old keets?

You may be able to buy a clutch of fertile eggs from a supplier and this will no doubt be cheaper than buying a minimum amount of day old keets. However, incubators can be expensive. Not to mention the time it will take to learn how to operate one properly, as well as the time needed for the actual incubation process.

### c) Incubating eggs if you already have an incubator

If you have an incubator because you are an experienced keeper of poultry, or you can borrow one from someone, then incubating a batch of eggs is a viable option. If however you are none of the above and are in fact a raw beginner, with no experience or equipment, then you are strongly advised to not consider this as an option.

### Advice and options on incubators to purchase

If having said all of that, you are very keen to learn how to incubate eggs, and have the time to spare necessary to manage the project, then the following advice will be helpful.

When you buy an incubator you generally have two options.

1. A basic still air model that has no automation and requires you to turn the eggs
2. An automated model that will have fan assisted ventilation with automatic egg turning.

If you have the time on your hands then number (1) is probably a good option for you as you will be on hand to turn the eggs 5 or 6 times per day. To say the least, this option is time consuming.

One of the disadvantages of this option is that you are also required to open the lid in order to complete the task. By doing this several times per day you are affecting both the humidity and temperature. If you are not careful this stop starting of temperature and humidity could easily affect your hatch rate. Another important disadvantage, of a still air unit is the still air. What can happen in these units is that not all of the incubator will be heated to the same temperature. Without going into a scientific explanation on thermal layers etc, with a still air incubator you are bound to get hot and cold parts that again could affect successful hatching. With an automatic air circulation unit, this will keep the temperature and humidity constant throughout.

If you live a busy lifestyle and are perhaps not available during the day, then the second option will probably be a must have.

### What type of unit should you use?

Unless you are a large producer who would use a large automated unit, you are likely to have a reasonably small unit. This would therefore not take up too much space and so you should try and accommodate this indoors. This would not only allow you to keep an eye on the progress, but ensure that adverse outside temperatures do not affect the internal temperature.

### d) Are cheaper incubators a good option?

Your choice of unit may well be determined by your budget. Even the cheapest units properly maintained and instructions carefully read and followed, should produce a successful hatch. If you get more serious about hatching, you can then maybe look at units that are more automated and fan assisted for example. Units are likely to vary depending on the unit you purchase. Fan assisted incubators are likely to operate for the duration of the incubation at approximately 99.5° F (37.5° C). Cheaper units that do not have automated air circulation and are therefore still air, operate around 102° F (38.9° C). These units also generally require that the temperature is taken higher than fan assisted. The thermometer bulb should in this case be in line with the top of the eggs. Again do not worry too much if you notice the temperature is more or less above and below the eggs. As long as you see a constant temperature where the eggs sit.

**To give you some idea of what you can expect, the following is a step by step guide to incubating the eggs**
Once you are familiar with the manufacturer instructions the actual process for incubation should be as follows; You should ideally have checked approximately how many eggs will fit into your particular incubator.

1.  Fill the water reservoirs and switch the unit on to start getting up to the required temperature, and humidity.

2.  Make sure that the stored eggs you intend to incubate are at room temperature. If you haven't already done so, draw a cross (preferably with a pencil), on one side of the egg.

3.  Once you are happy that the stored eggs are at room temperature and the incubator has reached optimum heat and humidity, carefully place the eggs in place, with the cross uppermost. Ensure you handle the eggs carefully and with clean, dry hands. Temperature is said to be best at 100° F (37.8° C), with a humidity of 50%.

4.  Do not add extra eggs once you start the incubation. It is possible with experience to add, for example chicken eggs, a week after you add the guinea eggs. Chicken eggs hatch after approximately 21 days, so they should hatch around the same time. What you want to avoid is opening the incubator once the keets from the first batch start hatching and adding more eggs. It is best to keep things simple, and not mix dates with temperature changes.

5. Once all the eggs are in place leave them but keep monitoring the required temperature and humidity as well as topping up the reservoirs with warm water.

6. From day one, also be aware that you are aiming to turn the eggs at least 5 or 6 times, and more if you can. Each time you do this, always avoid exposing the inside of the incubator for too long. If you can manage this on your own, lift the lid slightly and squeeze your hand into the incubator to turn the eggs. Avoid removing the lid altogether to do this, as the heat will escape and will take a while to heat up again. If you are not familiar with egg turning, this simply means as follows: You start with the cross uppermost, then the next time you turn, you place the cross face down, and alternating like this as you go.

7. This should now be your daily routine until day 26 – 28 when hatching begins.

8. At day 8 – 10 you can candle each egg to establish the fertile eggs from the clear infertile. Again we will talk more about this later.

9. Approximately 3 days before the eggs are due to hatch, you should stop turning the eggs as the keets need to be in position to begin hatching. The final 3 days of incubation, the humidity should be at 70% to 75%.

## 3) ADDITIONAL INFORMATION FOR INCUBATOR USE

### *What are the best conditions and location for your incubator?*

You should also try and locate the incubator where it will remain undisturbed throughout. A good room temperature for the incubator should be around 70° F (21°C). This is a comfortable temperature that is not too hot or cold. You should ensure it is not exposed to an extreme heat source, either hot or cold.

### *Testing the incubator*

Before starting any egg incubating, you should always run an incubator for at least a day or two to ensure it is running correctly and consistently. Of course if you are in any doubt as to the reliability of an incubator, do not commence the incubation.

### *Is it necessary to check the temperature regularly?*

Also check that your unit has an internal thermometer. In the unlikely event that it doesn't, you may have to place one inside and ensure the bulb is level with the egg. The reason for this is that as the air circulates the temperature may be slightly different at the top or bottom.

You should endeavor to keep the temperature as accurate as possible.

However, if you do find the temperatures fluctuating, the eggs are still likely to hatch, but either before or after the expected due date. You should be aware that guinea eggs can take up to 28 days to hatch, which as stated may be more or less.

### Temperature of the incubator

You will probably hear different recommendations from different breeders and keepers, for the correct temperature and humidity of the incubator. Some will say the temperature should be kept at 99.5°F (37.5° C). Others will tell you up to 103° F (39.4° C). The fact remains that a higher temperature will result in eggs hatching quicker. A lower temperature than 99.5°F (37.5° C), will no doubt take longer to hatch. In both cases, the results of the hatch may not be as favorable as for a steady 99.5°F (37.5° C). When you gain more experience, you may well decide to experiment with slight temperature variations, if you believe you could obtain better results. You should however, never attempt to overheat the incubator as this will probably result in cooking the eggs, or at the very least, a low hatch rate.

### Maintaining temperature during incubation

During incubation it is extremely important to maintain correct temperature of 37 to 38°C (98.6° F to 100.4° F) or to take its average 37.5° C (99.5° F). When storing eggs before incubation it is generally recommended that the temperature of the egg is kept below 68° F (20° C). When the temperature rises somewhat above this, then embryo development begins. If the temperature was again allowed to drop this again arrests development. This process is said to cause a gradual weakening of the embryo. Fluctuation of temperatures will not necessarily kill the embryo if the temperature is already at its optimum and then drops 5 or 10 degrees F, but it could possibly weaken it and therefore it cause the embryo to die.

### Taking the temperature of eggs

If you take the temperature underneath the eggs this should be approximately 97°F (36°C). Testing the temperature above the shell is likely to show a different temperature again. Testing for temperature is important as even the slightest difference can affect the keet, which could well die in the shell. Therefore always take the correct temperature recommended for your incubator, as long as it is along the guidelines mentioned here. Remember do not just take a general guideline, as guinea fowl need a higher temperature than chicks.

### Humidity

Again recommended humidity can vary depending on the unit. Some keepers assert that a humidity of 50 to 60% is ideal. Others will have had continued success at around 35 to 45 percent. However those that recommend lower humidity will suggest you need to raise this until 2 or 3 days before they are due to hatch. So on day 24 of a 26 day hatch you should increase the humidity to no less than 65%. The reason for raising the humidity in this case is that as the keets get ready to hatch and therefore move about more they are said to need more moisture. This is generally true of most chicks. But once again, regarding temperature or any other aspect, you should always check the instructions given for the unit you use.

### Why is humidity important?

Humidity levels should not be taken for granted. As the embryo develops, it is necessary for the internal liquid contents to be used up. If the humidity is too low then there is a risk that the internal egg contents will begin to dry up too quickly. There is therefore a risk of embryo dehydration and possible death. If the humidity level is extremely high then the internal liquid is not lost to a sufficient level and this can also cause complications.

As noted it is important that a correct humidity is established towards the end of the incubation period. This applies to natural as well as artificial incubation. It ensures that the egg shell does not become either too hard and brittle or too soft and rubbery that the keet has difficulty breaking through.

As well as temperature, humidity is important for the embryo development. You will notice that water reservoirs should be part of the unit. These need to be topped up all the time and should certainly never be allowed to dry out. If there isn't sufficient humidity and therefore moisture, the egg itself will eventually dry out. As you add water to the reservoirs, it is advised that this is not cold, but warm. As you can imagine, the cold water would soon cool the internal temperature. Also make sure that the reservoirs are placed below the mesh screen that the eggs rest on. You do not want to risk newly hatched chicks having access to a water pot, and accidentally falling in and drowning.

### What is the importance of ventilation?

You should be aware that the growing embryos need to dispel carbon dioxide ($CO_2$), and have a constant oxygen supply, ventilation is therefore vital. Again you should follow the instructions for your unit as to which vents to leave open or closed.

### Using colored water in the reservoir

**A tip if you are struggling to see the water level in the reservoir, that you are required to keep topped up for humidity, is to use a dye in the water.** Once again without this option you may be having to take the lid off unnecessarily. If you cannot get this from a specialist supplier, I would use a small amount of food coloring as a dilution. Certainly do not use any harmful chemical as this will contaminate the whole incubator. If in doubt, do not use any dye for coloring the water.

### What if there is a power cut during incubation?

If you are unfortunate enough to encounter a power cut at any time during incubation, you have a number of remedial options. You can hope the power returns after a couple of hours. Obviously better options are to have a spare incubator on hand that you can start up as soon as you can and transfer the eggs. Or you may have a generator that you can use until the power returns. You may also have a portable gas heater (please be aware with gas heaters there may be a risk with a faulty unit giving off carbon monoxide which could not only be dangerous to you, but could enter the unit), that would at least offer some level of heat until the power came back.

Also determine whether you think the internal incubator is getting sufficient ventilation and therefore oxygen. It may be necessary to open vents or perhaps allow ventilation into the room itself, if this appears stuffy. You could even consider taking the whole unit and placing it in your car. With the motor running and the heater on, you may find the incubator receives sufficient heat. Of course you would only want to attempt this outside and certainly not in an enclosed garage. The same goes for the generator, as the fumes given off would be very dangerous.

I would hope that you do not encounter such bad luck, but forewarned is forearmed.

### Cleaning the incubator

Whether you start your new batch with a brand new incubator or a used one, you should thoroughly clean the unit. A bleached based detergent or anti-bacterial solution should be used. As long as this is suitable to kill bacteria which may have been left after a previous use. What ever the detergent, you would of course thoroughly rinse with cold water, as detergent residue could have an adverse effect once you start in-

# BIRD EGG

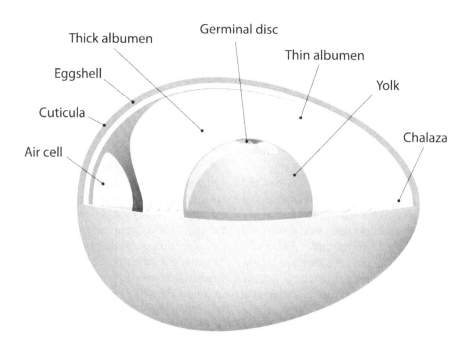

Thick albumen

Germinal disc

Thin albumen

Eggshell

Yolk

Cuticula

Chalaza

Air cell

cubating. The porous eggs could easily absorb the chemical and cause problems for the growing embryo.

## 4) EGGS INTENDED FOR HATCHING

### a) The egg structure

The structure of the egg is made up of thousands of microscopic pores. The function of this is to allow the intake of oxygen and the expulsion of carbon dioxide gases as the embryo develops. A drawback is that bacteria and other poisons can also enter the egg, causing growth problems or death to the embryo. The anatomy of the egg itself is basically made up of the egg yolk, germ spot attached to the egg yolk, egg white (albumen), air pocket, membrane and shell.

### b) Process of fertilization and egg production.

Basically, reproduction starts in one of the two ovaries of the female Guinea Fowl. Within this region, there are many *oocytes* or embryo eggs. Several of these *oocytes* develop into yolks until one passes into the *oviduct*. Once the male mates the female, his semen is passed into the *oviduct*, where the egg is fertilized. The development of the egg components such as the, albumen, membrane etc, start as secretions within the oviduct. Finally the egg passes to the cloaca, which the hen then lays. This process usually takes place within 24 hours.

### c) Development of the embryo

The development process starts with the germ spot or fertilized seed, which is where the keet originates. During incubation, an embryo develops and grows into the baby keet.

The purpose of the egg yolk is to offer the keet nourishment as it grows. The egg white initially protects the growing embryo from any accidental knocks and bumps. The egg white is also a source of food, later in the keets development. The air sack is the oxygen source for the keet.

### d) Egg shape and possible problems

If you were purchasing eggs from a professional hatchery, egg size and quality should not be noticeably different. If you were selecting eggs from your own birds to incubate, you may come across eggs of differing sizes. The normal Guinea Fowl egg, should be more conical than oval, i.e. one end is quite pointed, whereas the other end is quite rounded. The shape of the egg is therefore said to indicate the health and any heredity defects of either the hen used or the cock used for fertilization. This isn't to say that slight differences in shape will produce offspring that are defective. But it has been found that abnormally shaped eggs may either not hatch at all or produce keets that may unfortunately show weaknesses or defects. It is fair to say that a small egg will undoubtedly have a small yolk. This may well produce a keet which is undernourished and underdeveloped.

### What if eggs have a crack in them?

You should also be careful not to incubate eggs that appear cracked as you may find these do not hatch, or develop problems.

# BIRD EMBRYO

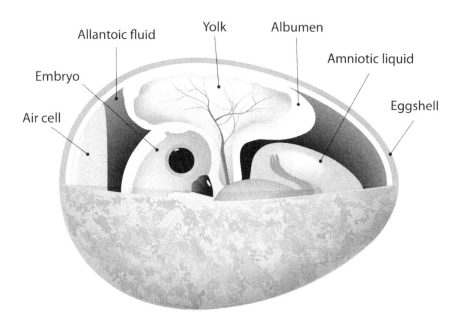

Allantoic fluid    Yolk    Albumen

Amniotic liquid

Embryo

Eggshell

Air cell

### e) Importance of collecting eggs for incubating

It is also recommended that the eggs are collected as soon after the egg is laid, preferably within 4 hrs, and placed under the recommended cooling temperature not exceeding 68° F (20° C) and not falling below 50° F (10° C). The important point of this is to avoid the stop start of embryo development, which is thought to contribute to a lower hatch rate.

### f) What temperature should eggs for incubating be stored at?

Again, eggs for hatching should be stored in a place that has a temperature not exceeding 68° F (20° C) and not falling below 50° F (10° C). In controlled conditions such as professional hatcheries, the ideal optimum temperature range is said to be between 55° F and 61° F (13° C to 16° C). Under normal circumstances they should not be in a dry environment, and if you suspect this may be the case, check that humidity is between 70 and 80%.

### g) How long should you store eggs

Eggs for incubation should be as fresh as possible. Usually eggs over 7 - 10 days have a lower hatch rate. It seems to be the case that the longer the eggs are stored the greater the chance of a decreased hatch rate. Some breeders have suggested that you should endeavor to incubate eggs less than 7 days after they are laid, and certainly no more than 7 days. Experiments have suggested that there is a decrease of approximately 4% in hatch-ability for every day that the egg is stored. The most recently laid eggs will rapidly develop, and certainly faster than older eggs. Once the fertilized egg starts to develop in most cases this continues without any trouble. However, there is a significant percentage that die or develop complications and these usually occur around day 4 and day 25. As the egg gets older it can become stale and reduce the chances of a successful hatch. Again it is debatable whether eggs that are say 10 to 14 days old or more will not hatch. But it is generally recommended that eggs for incubating should be kept for no more than 10 days. The best results are obtained the fresher the eggs are. Any eggs that you purchase from a hatchery or your own may not be exactly the same age. In most cases this should not be a problem, but the older the egg gets the more likely it is that problems with hatch rate could occur.

## h) Recording dates eggs

The important thing as far as eggs for incubating, is to store them safely and correctly, but to also keep a record of how old they are. Some people do not bother with this, but it is a good idea to write the date on each egg, use a pencil rather than an ink marker. If you have many eggs that you keep in separate boxes, label the box with the date collected.

## i) Dirty eggs and incubating

Eggs that are intended for incubation and are dirty should be cleaned with a course material cloth. Anything too abrasive such as sand paper should be avoided as this can damage the surface cuticle of the egg.

If disinfecting the eggs is necessary then this should preferably take place soon after the egg is laid. The egg at this point should still be warm and should ideally not have cooled. When the egg cools, the internal contents actually contract and at the same time any bacteria will be drawn into the egg.

## Should you clean eggs before incubation

Eggs that you purchase from a supplier should be clean. If one or two have some dirt, then be careful not to wash these in the conventional sense. The egg shell is porous as you know, and is made up of a matrix of thousands of tiny holes. Any dirt left on the egg that is allowed to become damp could easily penetrate the egg and contaminate the inside. Having said that, you might mistakenly wash or wipe dirty eggs, and have no problems hatching, but it is a risk that should be avoided. As mentioned, a good method for removing dry dirt, an abrasive pad and lightly brush the shell until clean. The problem with putting dirty eggs in the incubator is that the incubator requires humidity as well as heat. Bacteria from feces can reactivate and possibly contaminate the whole incubator.

## What else you should know about stored eggs?

For actually containing the stored eggs, some people make wooden trays lined with sawdust to store the eggs, or use plastic trays similar to bakers trays. You should also be aware that these stored eggs need to be turned on a daily basis. This is something all birds do naturally in the wild. The purpose for this is to prevent a lop sided development and ensure the yolk does not stick to one side of the shell. As previously mentioned, the most common way to turn eggs is to draw a cross on one side, preferably using a pencil. You simply lay the egg on a flat surface with the pointed end and blunt end parallel to the surface. You then draw the cross on the uppermost part. So on the first day the cross is facing upwards. You then turn it the next time, so the cross is touching the surface. You then repeat the next time, when the cross will be at the top again, and so on.

### How many times per day do you need to turn the eggs?

There are a number of recommendations for how many times you should do this on a daily basis. Approximately half a dozen times is a good estimate. If you have to leave the unit whilst you go to work, it may be a good idea to ask a friend or neighbor to pop in mid day to do this for you. You can then turn them at least once in the morning and as many as four times over the rest of the evening until you retire for the evening. Some keepers will advise only needing to turn the eggs a minimum of 2 times a day. This may well be adequate, but you are strongly advised to turn them as many as 6 times.

### Why is egg turning necessary?

As previously mentioned, the hen will naturally turn the eggs and she will do this approximately every 20 to 30 minutes.

The author of the following article *http://dev.biologists.org/content/5/3/293.full.pdf* Suggests that in a 24 hour period this was noted at 96 times. Anyone particularly interested in the findings of this scientific study should consult that article.

Having said that, of all the studies and experiments into the phenomenon of egg turning, lack of egg turning led to yolks adhering to the shell, lack of sufficient nutrition for the growing embryo, malformed chicks and possible death.

Whatever the specific scientific reasons why we need to turn eggs, the hen does this by nature and therefore you need to follow the natural course of action.

### Turning eggs in a still air incubator

Hand turning of still air incubator eggs should be done at least 5 or 6 times a day for 10 days. After which it is said that this only needs to be done 3 times per day, and this is up to the 24th day. Even though it is usually estimated that the eggs will begin hatching between the 26th and 28th day, it is usual for eggs to hatch at the 27th. At the 24th day, this gives the eggs at least 2 days of non turning, but more likely 3 days.

As a routine, check the humidity level is correct when you turn the eggs and adjust accordingly.

### Should you incubate different poultry breeds together?

If you are in a position to have eggs from different breeds that you would like to hatch, then it is possible, but can be complicated. If you do not have a problem juggling the different temperature, humidity and hatching time, then fine.

Here is an example of different hatch rates. The guinea egg hatches between 26 and 28 days and a chicken egg starts to hatch after 20 days, and goose eggs 28 to 32 days. So you can see from that factor alone, you would have to stagger when you start which eggs. And that isn't even taking into consideration, any temperature or humidity differences. Also the cooler eggs that you introduce, or the disruption when you start to remove hatching chicks, will affect the temperature, which needs to be constant throughout. If you decide to attempt something like this at any point, it probably will not be a disaster, but you are likely to have a lower hatch rate.

### When not to incubate eggs?

Although not impossible, it is not advised to start incubating a clutch of eggs beyond late August. The reason for this is that by the time the keets hatch, the weather will be changing and getting cooler. Ideally the keets should be fully feathered towards October at the latest.

### Why you need to remove eggs suspected of being bad or infertile?

If you should notice a nasty odor coming from the incubator, this is likely to be a bad egg that should be removed immediately. You should not under normal circumstances suffer any nasty odors from the incubator during the incubation process.

## 5) CANDLING: CHECKING EGGS ARE FERTILE

### A) HOW WILL YOU KNOW IF THE EGGS ARE FERTILE

In the space of a couple of days of male/female copulation, fertilization of eggs takes place. Unless the process from day one is studied under a microscope, there is no way of knowing at what point and if an egg has been successfully fertilized.

You may find that some eggs you incubate will not be fertile, and will therefore remain clear. Most of them however, will develop and hatch. Unless you leave the eggs to their own devises until they start to hatch, the only sure way of knowing is by candling. Candling is basically done by placing the egg over a strong light.

Candling is a recommended procedure that you carry out on an egg between 7 and 10 days. Certainly by day 10 you will have a very good idea if early embryonic development is taking place. Under the strong light, you should be able to see a network of blood vessels throughout the egg. If the egg didn't at least have this showing, and appeared clear, the egg is probably infertile and will therefore not develop into an embryo.

The thickness of the Guinea Fowl shell can make candling less easy. Which is why a strong light and waiting around 10 days, may be necessary to see if there is positive embryo growth.

Candling is another situation where different people suggest candling at different times. So you will hear some advise to candle after 7 days, or 10 days is the best time, some even 14 days. An inexperienced person should be able to

tell if there has been some development by day 10. If you cannot be certain by the 10th day, then have another look in 4 or 5 days time.

**TIP:** When candling be careful to open and close the lid as quickly as possible, to retain the temperature inside.

## B) HOW DOES CANDLING WORK?

Ultra violet candling lights are used for the purposes of candling, as these can effectively penetrate the thicker shell of the Guinea Fowl. Sometimes it is advisable to candle the eggs initially before starting incubation, in order to check for hair line cracks. At 7 to 10 days candling of a fertile egg should show up as a darkened globule. 10 to 14 days after this, further inspection should show a marked increase in size of the embryo. If you see no significant growth from the previous candling, the embryo is probably dead.

### c) WHAT DO YOU NEED TO LOOK FOR WHEN CANDLING?

If you are unsure what you are looking for, purchase or borrow a candling torch and place a standard shop bought chicken egg over it. What you see under the light is what is known as clear and you should be able to make out the yolk, egg white and air sack. Again, after 7 – 10 days of incubating your Guinea Fowl eggs, you will hopefully see a dark shadow. This will indicate that the egg was originally fertilized and you now have a growing keet embryo.

### *Candling problems and what to look for*

If you candle the eggs and you find many eggs are clear there could be a number of possible causes. Firstly ensure the candling torch that you use is strong enough and therefore suitable for Guinea Fowl eggs. Remember that the shell is thicker than a chicken egg, and so will need a stronger light. It could be because you have candled too early to be able to see any noticeable signs of embryo growth. Or it could be a sign that the hen is too young or old. There may be a problem with her reproductive system. The cock may be too young or old or over worked, and his sperm count is too low.

If you notice obviously clear, infertile eggs, you can remove these as there is no use keeping them in the incubator. Again, as the eggs develop a dark shadow will gradually take over the egg until only the air sack will be visible. This indicates that the keet is growing healthily inside.

During the initial candling any eggs that appear to be cracked or leaking should be discarded, as these are unlikely to develop. At worse such egg can leak into the incubator and contaminate the inside as well as the other eggs. Also eggs that appear clear after the second candling should be removed. For the same reason if subsequent candling reveals eggs that showed initial development then stopped, they are likely to be dead. With any of the eggs that are likely to be bad in some way, there is a risk they can explode and contaminate the inside of the incubator and consequently the good eggs.

# Chapter Eight

# Breeding: The Hatch Begins

This chapter covers what you can expect when the kkets start to hatch. You will also find information about hatching eggs with a broody hen.

# 1) WHAT TO EXPECT WHEN THE HATCH BEGINS

## a) When will the eggs hatch?

With optimum temperature, humidity and a healthy growing embryo, keets should start to hatch between 26 and 28 days, with an average at day 27. Do not be surprised if you are waiting over 30 days for some eggs to hatch. It does happen and you should therefore not be in a rush to discard eggs that have not hatched after 28 days.

## b) Keets Hatching; What you need to know

By day 25 the baby keet is in the hatching position, usually opposite the pointed end. The first thing the baby keet does is perforate the air sack, which full of oxygen, stimulates the lungs to start working. The keet immediately begins creating its first air hole through the egg. The next 48 hours will be the most arduous of the young birds life up until that point.

With the egg tooth, which is the tooth like protrusion on the top of the keet or chicks beak, the keets will start 'pipping' i.e. chipping at the shell to break out. You should not worry unduly if some keets seem to break out within a couple of hours and others take much longer. Each baby keet will take as long as it needs. In some cases this can take up to 2 days to complete.

## Opening the ventilation vents in a still air incubator

Once the keets start to hatch you are generally advised to allow additional ventilation into the incubator. The emerging keets will certainly need more oxygen at this stage, and this should not affect the keets still hatching.

## Problems with keets hatching

Weaker keets that struggle to hatch, should be helped if it looks as if they will need your help. In many cases a struggling keet may take a rest for a while, because it is exhausted, but will continue. Keets that you help should be monitored as for the first few days, they may need special help and attention. These keets can prove to be strong and healthy if given the chance. I would never recommend leaving a struggling keet to die if you can at all help it. If it dies later, then at least you did all you could to help.

## What if the keets are struggling with the hatch?

There is debate as to whether you should help a keet that seems to be struggling. Sometimes they will die anyway because of natural weakness or exhaustion. You may wish to help a keet that has been hatching out longer than a day. Sometimes with care, they will thrive and grow along with the others. At other times and with all your best efforts they will die anyway. After about 2 days any that do not seem to be showing any signs of pipping may well be dead inside the shell. I personally would leave them a bit longer just in case.

## Egg shells stuck to the keet

If you notice shells stuck to the keet, you can do one of two things.

1. Leave the shell to naturally fall off.
2. Use a warm water solution to soften the dried matter and

gently remove the shell that way.

Either way, you should never attempt to just pull this off. You could easily tear the skin of the keet causing it to bleed, and possibly get infected.

### c) What should you do once the keets have hatched?

It is said that the newly hatched keet has nourishment to last up to 70 hours, but food should be introduced no later than 40. In most cases it should be made available within 24 hours whether the keets attempts to eat this or not.

The keets that are the first to hatch will be wet but will soon dry from the heat of the incubator. Eventually they will resemble the little balls of fluff day old chick that you have no doubt seen in the past. The keets can remain in the incubator as long as they need to dry out. It is unlikely that all the keets will hatch at the same time. So a couple of hours after they hatch and appear dry, you can start to remove them from the incubator and into the brooder.

### Fluid intake after hatching

Within the first few days, it is important that the keets have sufficient

fluid intake. If you remember that they have just left the incubator and were kept at a high humidity level of around 80%. A sudden drop in moisture can result in rapid dehydration.

### What is an expected hatch rate?

Commercial hatcheries make claims of hatch rates of approximately 95%. These large enterprises run extremely precise systems, where everything is controlled from temperature and humidity, to strict artificial insemination procedures. So do not be surprised if you experience a hatch rate that is much less.

### What hatch rate can you expect?

You will have done extremely well if you have a 100% successful hatch rate. Most hatches have at least a few infertile or partially developed embryos that die for whatever reason.

An average success rate will be somewhere between 50% and 75%, and of course you will experience or hear of fluctuations beyond those figures.

### Problems with hatching

Providing you follow the guidelines for optimum results then you should have a high percentage of eggs that develop and hatch. If you have recurrent problems then the following suggestions may be worth a try. It is a good idea if you can, to identify which eggs come from which hen. You can create a simple spread sheet or even a notebook and create codes for each hen. You can then monitor any batches of eggs that are consistently clear. If this occurs with many hens then it is possible the cock guinea is at fault and may need replacing. Obviously if you identify one hen then you would be as well to use her eggs for consumption only.

### Hatching problems associated with high temperature

Higher temperatures than those recommended seem to cause problems relating to the heart, circulation and nervous system. There also seems to be an associated risk of drying out in particular if the humidity is not sufficiently adjusted to match the increased temperature. It is perhaps the case that the hatch rate will be better if the temperature is lower than it should be rather than too high. But even then the lower temperature can cause abnormal or stunted growth as well as heart and circulatory problems.

## 2) HATCHING WITH A BROODY HEN

Allowing the guinea hen to incubate her eggs

At some point you may decide to allow the Guinea hen to incubate her own eggs and therefore not collect the eggs. Do not be surprised to see a clutch of 25 to 30 eggs in one nest. Guinea fowl in the same way as other poultry have a tendency to use the same nest, so the eggs are probably from more than one hen.

### a) Guinea hens sitting eggs

Guinea Hens seem to be dedicated brooders of eggs in the wild and generally make attentive parents both wild and domesticated. However, in enclosed domestic surrounding, they seem to be much more prone to unreliability and will abandon a nest for no apparent reason after a couple of weeks.

They can also be put off sitting eggs if at some point during the incubation they experience adverse weather conditions. For this reason some keepers prefer to use either a broody hen or an incubator. You would not necessarily need to collect the eggs daily for incubation purposes. What you do not want to do however, is to put the guinea hen off laying in the nest that you know about.

### *What role does the hen and cock play in incubating and brooding eggs?*

In the wild, whilst the Guinea hen will sit and incubate the eggs, the male is said to take over to brood the newly hatched keets. It is not uncommon for him to do this for the majority of the time until they sufficiently mature. The keets are usually fully feathered by six weeks of age. It is not uncommon for them to have sufficient strength to start taking short flights within a couple of weeks.

### *b) Keets raised by a broody hen*

One advantage of keets raised by a guinea hen who is part of the flock is that the keets get instant acceptance.

### *Are broody hens a good option for incubating eggs?*

Broody bantams and chickens generally provide more reliability when naturally hatching eggs. As bantams are smaller than chickens, ensure that the clutch you give her to sit is not too many that she cannot comfortably cover them. As the guinea eggs are smaller than chicken, a bantam or small chicken should be able to cover around 15 to 20 eggs. Larger hens could possibly manage double this amount.

### *The best broody hens*

As well as turkey hens the best foster mothers tend to be Silkies, or silkie crosses. Buff Orpington, and the like also do well, and can realistically cover around 12 eggs. If crossed with for example a Sussex or Rhode Island chicken, then these provide the dependability of the silkie and the size of the other larger chicken. These birds should easily be able to cover up to around 18 guinea fowl eggs. A turkey hen will obviously manage more than this.

### Incubating eggs under a broody hen

Suggested number of eggs for a broody hen would be approximately 15 eggs for a reasonable size hen and up-to 10 eggs for a bantam.

Depending on the size of the broody bantam, up to 12 eggs should be a comfortable amount for her to sit. Remember that she needs to comfortably cover all the eggs. So when you place the eggs into a nest make sure that when she sits them, none are visible. If you see any that are poking out, you should remove them as soon as you can. They will probably go cold and not develop anyway. It is better to have too few and therefore have a greater chance of a successful hatch.

### Fitness of the broody hen

You should check that any prospective broody hen is fit and healthy. You will probably see instantly if she looks ill, but she should basically appear bright and vital. Some breeders even recommend sprinkling louse powder on her feathers and the nest box, to kill any parasites likely to affect her health for the duration of the incubation and brooding period. If you have never seen a broody hen, you will tell instantly as she acts much different to her normal behavior. These hens generally ruffle their feathers and cluck all the time, sometimes the other birds peck at her.

### Making a suitable nest for the broody hen

The nest that you make should form a concave cavity. Some keepers make a shallow box, approximately 1 to 1.5 ft square (30.5 cm to 45.7 cm square) and approximately 4 inches (10.2 cm) high. Layer the bottom with sawdust or shavings and then pack the box with soft straw or hay. You can of course do the same thing on the ground. If the base of the area is soil you can dig a hollow, or use a turf of grass to make the shape and line it the same way.

### Using a grass sod

Some keepers also recommend using an earth or grass sod, to make the nest for the eggs. The advantage of this is that providing the sod is moist, but not overly damp, it will help retain the humidity of the eggs. It is also a good idea to moisten this with some sprinkled water if it looks to be drying out. As with incubation in an incubator, this is particularly important after the third week when a greater humidity is required.

### Brooding pen to accommodate a broody hen

Please note that the following information is a suggestion for a pen enclosure that the brooder box then goes into.

The area needs to be large enough that the hen and keets can move with ease. You certainly do not want it so cramped that there is a risk the hen stands on any of the keets and injures them.

You can either make a purpose built pen, or convert a suitable area. Either way, the brooder should ideally be enclosed within a fenced off or caged surround.

Some people choose to use a pen or cubicle that is approximately 4 or 5 ft (1.2 or 1.5 meters) wide, by 5 or 6ft (1.5 or 1.8 meters) long, by 6 ft (1.8 meters)high. The sides and the ceiling can be made from plywood sheets or something similar to create a solid draft free partition.

It is best if the front is mostly wire mesh, similar to an aviary. Make sure that there is a door way or hatch that you can get in and out. You may wish to make the door the full dimensions which would be 6 ft (1.8 meters) high by 4 or 5 ft (1.2 meters 1.5 meters) wide. By doing this you can easily get a brooder in and out. Otherwise you will have to construct and dismantle it in-situ.

The importance of having the front of the main cubicle made of wire is so that other adult birds that may be in the hen house can have full view of the new keets and the broody hen.

## What you should do whist a broody hen is sitting eggs

Whilst a broody hen is incubating the eggs you are advised to not disturb her unless you have to. There is certainly no need to worry unduly as she will be doing everything she has to. Once the keets start to hatch you may see egg shells appear which you can remove. As with incubator hatchings, this can take 2 days before all the keets that are likely to hatch, will hatch. You should ensure that the hen has water if she needs it, but many advise against feeding her during the 48 hour period, when the eggs start to hatch.

## Broody hens leaving the nest

When a broody hen leaves a nest, you may worry that she has gone too long and it may affect the embryos if they cool. However, an experiment was carried out to test this under controlled conditions. In this case the temperature was lowered by 41°F (5°C), twice a day for half an hour each time. Remarkably the results showed an improvement up to 5% in the hatch rate.

## Exercising the hen

You should allow the hen to exercise at least once per day, and food, water and grit should be available for her. This should ideally be done at roughly the same time. She will only leave the eggs for 10 or 15 minutes and will return in time, before they have a chance of chilling.

## In the wild You have been successful with the preceding, now what?

Once the chicks start hatching you should proceed as you would if you were transferring the keets from the incubator to the brooder. But remember there is no need to transfer them at this stage as the mother will be providing the warmth. However you should ideally prepare a brooder unit and soon after, place the keets in there. they will need a food and water supply. Unless it is practical to provide separate food for the hen, you may find that you are feeding both the hen and chicks with the starter food. It would be difficult to prevent her from eating that anyway. after

## What you should do once the broody

### *hen has hatched the eggs*

The broody hen will show the keets food and water and do not be too surprised to see them feeding within 24 hours of hatching. While you are feeding the keets chick crumb or turkey starter, you should supplement the hen's diet with a small handful of corn or wheat. Also do not forget that she will need access to grit in order to process any grain you give her.

### *Broody hen*

A broody hen is an excellent way of introducing the young keets to the rest of the flock. As with most young offspring, the baby keets will imprint, that is identify with the other birds and assume they are one and the same.

The guinea fowl natural wild and noisy tendency can at least be reduced by raising them from keets. The other advantage of a broody hen is that they will to a large extent imprint on her and copy what she does. So they will follow her and feed like her, and most importantly follow her into the hen house to roost. You certainly do not want them to be influenced by any semi wild adult guinea fowl that have a predisposition to roost in trees.

### *Selling or giving away your day old keets*

If at any point you intend to give away or sell surplus keets, you should ensure they are feeding and drinking first, which should be within the day of hatching.

## 3) HATCHING WITH A BROODY HEN IN THE WILD

### a) Overview of the Guinea hens egg laying season

Guinea fowl hens will generally lay eggs anywhere from the beginning of March to the end of September. Guinea fowl are not like chickens, who will readily lay their eggs in a nesting box. Guinea fowl may well lay their eggs in a nesting box, but are more inclined to lay outside in a secluded area, or under a bush. They are known to lay on the ground, so if you decide to incorporate nest boxes in the hen house, you should make sure some are at ground level. You may find by doing this, more guinea hens will lay in the boxes anyway. Guinea fowl have a tendency to lay eggs in the same nest as others. So it is unlikely that if you find a clutch of 30 eggs or so after a few weeks, that one hen has laid them. Once a nest has accumulated this amount of eggs, you will find one of the hens goes broody. She will then start to incubate the eggs and at approximately 26 days the eggs will start to hatch.

### b) Looking for secluded nests, free range.

Once again, not all Guinea hens will want to lay eggs in man made boxes and will prefer laying in the wild if possible. This can be a problem and you should be aware that if the hens are free ranging, you need to find any secluded nests if you can. The hen will be very vulnerable to predator attack, and you could well lose her and any eggs or keets.

A good way to detect a secluded nest is to watch the cock birds. They are likely to loiter in the area where the hen is sitting in order to protect her. This can also be detrimental to them

as it can alert a predator to where the hen is to be found. You also need to realize that the hen will incubate her eggs throughout the night. So if she is out in the open, she is at even more risk of a predator attack. It is therefore desirable to encourage her to lay in the hen house or at least somewhere that you know about.

### c) Should you allow your guinea fowl hen to incubate her own eggs?

You may decide to allow a guinea hen to lay and sit her own eggs out in the wild, however, I would only recommend this if she was in a safe enclosure. We will talk more about this shortly. She will probably lay her clutch in the same nesting spot.

Guinea hens, although capable, are not the most reliable mothers. If she is disturbed she could easily abandon a nest, and obviously once the temperature of the eggs drops for a prolonged period, they will die. You need to remember that it doesn't take much to upset a guinea hen and for her to abandon a nest. Even if you were to manage to get her into your hen house she may not continue sitting. She may also be too distressed and agitated that you would have probably been best attempting to incubate the eggs yourself. Or on the off chance you have a broody hen you could use.

Incidentally, when you start collecting eggs, if you intend some for hatching, it is not advised to collect all the eggs that you find in any nest. If the hen returns to an empty nest, she may instinctively abandon that nest for a new one. You should therefore leave approximately 6 eggs in the nest to encourage her to continue. Some keepers advocate replacing the actual eggs with pot eggs or something similar.

### What happens if a hen hatches a clutch of eggs?

As mentioned she could for whatever reason abandon the nest at whatever stage of incubation the eggs are at. Once the eggs are hatched however, Guinea Fowl instinctively abandon the nest for fear of attracting predators. As the eggs do not generally hatch at the same time, she may leave eggs that are in the initial stages of hatching. The keets that have survived the hatch will be expected to follow the mother immediately and become chilled and die in the process. If the grass is long and damp, the keets will soon get damp also, and soon get chilled. Even in warm weather, she may march the young keets to exhaustion. Under these circumstances they can soon dehydrate if they do not get to a water supply.

Obviously guinea hens have no choice in the wild, and it could be argued that they manage perfectly well. But I personally would not like to take this risk and prefer safer more controlled methods.

### What should you do if you discover a nest?

If you come across a clutch of eggs that appear to be in the process of incubation, there are a number of points to bear in mind.

A nest that apparently appears abandoned may not be. Guinea hens are known to leave a nest in search of food and water, and she will likely return within 15 or 20 minutes.

### A cage to protect her

If you leave the hen to incubate the eggs, it would be advisable to construct a makeshift cage. This would be no different to isolating her in a pen or cage within the hen house. Some people advocate, taking something like a pet cage, and providing you can remove one side, simply place this over the hen. This needs to be done carefully and quickly, as you do not want to disturb her and frighten her off the nest. If she bolts, you can either catch her and put her back on the nest. Or perhaps you may decide that the best thing is to incubate the eggs in an incubator. If you have to do this then please remember that you do not want to leave the eggs exposed for longer than 15 or 20 minutes. If something like this does happen, be sure to cover the clutch with something to insulate them with, such as a woolen blanket.

If you have the option to use a cage it would be advisable to anchor the cage if you can, in case a predator does find her and tries to upturn the cage. I would also want to create a fence around the cage. You only need to make this approximately 6 foot square (0.6 m²).

### She will need food and water

If you are successful in putting a cage or something similar over her, you will have to provide her with food and water. She will obviously not be able to leave the cage for the duration.

### Mother and babies: Keets hatched naturally in the wild

If a hen appears with a clutch of baby keets in tow, you are well advised to round them up/herd them, and keep them in your enclosure. This is for obvious safety reasons because of potential predator attacks.

It may also be necessary if the weather isn't favorable and there is a risk that the keets may get wet and chilled and possibly die. You also need to ensure the keets are receiving sufficient nutritious feed.

### Herding mother and keets

If you do therefore round them up, be careful not to frighten them, as the keets in particular will be skittish and wary. If you can, leave the door to the run open and tempt the mother in with white millet or some other treat. If this doesn't work, you may have to drive them in from behind, but again do not rush them, and preferably seek help from other people. You are very unlikely to catch them by hand, so try and avoid this as you will certainly frighten the keets. If the keets go missing as a result of this, they could quickly lose body heat and die.

### In the wild if all else fails

As mentioned previously perhaps a better alternative is to prepare an area in the hen-house or somewhere you can accommodate her undisturbed. You will have to catch her, and collect the eggs (be very careful with these and make sure you have a suitable container with a soft base, so they do not roll about or bump each other). If you have any hope of this working you will need to keep the eggs warm and obviously act as quickly as possible. You may not have time to do anything elaborate here, but attempt to have some sort of a nest. If you are using the aforementioned cage, or even

a pen, make sure you bed this out with soft straw and shavings. You can hollow a nest in one corner approximately 1ft x 1ft (35 cm x 35 cm). Then carefully replace the eggs, and the hen. Hopefully she will continue to sit the eggs immediately. Again you will need to provide her with water and food.

Some people like the idea of allowing the hen to sit her own eggs free range. Once again, I would only attempt this if it were possible to have a secure cage over her that is approximately 2 cubic foot. This would need to be pegged down so that it could not be up turned. There is also debate as to whether you have some sort of opening in this cage that allows her to leave and exercise.

Again, it is a matter of preference as to what to do in these situations. Some people prefer to let nature take its course and others prefer to intervene and transfer hen and eggs to a safe place in the coop. There is no easy solution to this as both are fraught with possible complications. Hopefully the preceding has prompted you towards avoiding the hen brooding eggs free range. Again, hopefully it has also given you a few options of how to deal with this if you have no choice.

# CHAPTER NINE

# AFTER HATCHING: THE BROODER

Whichever method of hatching has been used, the keets will need some type of brooding. This is naturally taken care of by a broody hen. But if the eggs were hatched in an incubator, you will need a brooder. This chapter gives you information about the brooder as well as feeding, water and keeping the keets warm.

# 1) BROODER REQUIREMENTS

## A) WHEN SHOULD YOU PREPARE THE BROODER?

Once hatching has begun, or if you are getting them from a hatchery, you should prepare the brooder. In case you do not know, the brooder is the place you transfer the newly hatched keets. In essence, the brooder provides a safe, warm, dry environment that allows them to live, when they are at their most vulnerable.

The brooder should be set up in advance, which should have already been cleaned and disinfected. The brooder ideally needs to be running at an optimum heat before you introduce the keets. Ideally this needs to have been for approximately 24 hours. Unless a broody hen is used, a heat lamp is usually in place as the keets will need to retain a comfortable body temperature and certainly not be allowed to chill. On the 27th day of incubation or the day before your hatchery keets arrive, switch the brooder on so that it can warm up. If keets have started to hatch before the 27th day, then switch on as they start to hatch.

What type of brooder do you need?

Brooders can either be purchased as ready made units or you can construct your own. You have a number of options with brooders, such as wood, cardboard or plastic. Plastic is probably the most practical as it is the easiest to clean and disinfect and is relatively light. Wood is a common choice as an option for the DIY person. Cardboard can be a viable option as a quick fix, temporary, last resort. I would only recommend cardboard if you need something in a hurry. They tend not to be the best option in terms of hygiene. There is also a fire risk from a lamp been too close to the cardboard. Also the fact that cardboard can easily become damp and easily collapse.

## B) WHAT IF YOUR KEETS WERE BOUGHT FROM A HATCHERY?

Once you receive the keets, they will need to be placed in the brooder as soon as they arrive. Do not be surprised if one or two keets have expired when you open the box. This can be distressing, but it is an unfortunate fact that they may have been overwhelmed with the stress of the journey. With this in mind you should also not be surprised if the keets seem quiet and inactive at first. This should not last long, as the keets will soon recover from the exhaustion of the journey, and be full of spirit in no time.

## C) SHOULD THE BROODER/PEN, BE IN THE MAIN COOP?

If you already have mature birds, and it is possible to safely accommodate the brooder in the same area, then this will also help greatly with socializing. If you use this method then be sure that the keets are safe and the older birds cannot physically contact them. You certainly want to avoid older birds attacking the young, vulnerable keets. The safest method it to have a segregated pen inside the hen-house that the brooder can go into. You will then have double safety. The idea is that the older birds can see the keets and get familiar with them and the keets see everything that goes on in the new surroundings.

## 2) BROODER CONSTRUCTION

### A) MAKING YOUR OWN BROODER

If you cannot afford a ready-made brooder or would prefer to make one yourself, my advice would be to make a simple construction out of plywood. I would also suggest making this in two sections. The two sections basically comprise an internal part that will have a heat source. The heat source will be necessary when the temperature drops. The second section is an outside part that gives the keets more space to wander about or perhaps cool off.

For any reader wishing to build their own brooder, I have included what are considered to be recommended dimensions and space needed for keets. However, I have purposely not included how to actually build a brooder as this can get complicated and opinions differ on how to do this. You will also find very useful existing resources for this by simply searching Google for [building a brooder] such as the following

***http://www.backyardchick-ens.com/a/homemade-chicken-brooder-designs-pictures***

There are also some excellent videos on You-tube, that go into detail on how to build a brooder.

Brooder size is obviously dependent on the amount of keets you wish to accommodate. There is no easy answer but a generous rule of thumb is 50 inches squared $(50"^2)$ for each bird. This would mean an area that is 5 inches by 10 inches for each bird. So if we said that we have to accommodate 30 birds and each needs $50"^2$ then $50 \times 30 = 1500"^2$ which in feet squared terms is $10ft^2$ ap-

prox. This would mean dimensions for a brooder of 2ft x 5ft (0.6 meters x 1.5 meters approx) or 3ft 2" x 3ft 2" approx (1 meter x 1 meter approx). So if you only need enough space for 10 birds then narrow the dimensions for 30 to a realistic size for a third of that amount. So we could say for 2ft x 5ft, rather than be too precise, use workable dimensions of 1ft x 2 ft. Or for 20 birds say 2ft x 4ft. I personally would not recommend however purposely making or purchasing a brooder that is less than 2ft x 4ft, even if you only need to accommodate 10 keets. 2ft x 4ft is more practical to use again, and at a push you could accommodate 30 keets in a brooder of that size. Please bare in mind that this brooder is only necessary for the first 2 weeks.

### B) FLOOR SPACE NECESSARY INSIDE THE BROODER AS THE KEETS GROW.

However, this is were it gets more complicated. When the keets are small and fluffy, they do not take up much space at all. But as they grow, the dimensions given above will all of a sudden seem very restricted.

So the following offers a rough guideline as to how much space the keets are likely to need each week. Recommended space depending on the age of the keet is as follows.

» Between week 1 and week 6, up to 18 keets per 1 meter squared. (3ft 2" x 3ft 2" approx)

» At week 7, up to 16 keets per 1 m². (3ft 2" x 3ft 2" approx)

» At week 8, up to 14 keets per 1 m².

» At week 9, up to 12 keets per 1 m².

» At week 10, up to 11 keets per 1 m².

» At week 11, up to 10 keets per 1 m².

» At week 12, up to 9 keets per 1 m².

### *Floor covering inside the brooder and c) pen*

Please be aware that the floor needs to be covered in a non-slip material. At first the keets are relatively fragile and this includes their legs. It can be so easy for them to slip accidentally and damage a leg, possibly a breakage. It is therefore recommended to cover the floor with something like sawdust, shredded paper or soft shaving, or some combination of this. You should make sure that this is clean and dry at all times. Do not make this too deep as you do not want to bury the keets. Make sure that any litter does not get into the drinking dispenser. You will have to clean this out of the drink dispenser initially but as the keets grow you can raise this up by placing it on a block. If you do this, make sure the keets can still reach in and that it is sturdy enough and it doesn't topple over. Remember that as you should be aiming to provide fresh clean water on a daily basis, you are as well to clean this out daily anyway.

However, some keepers prefer to use news paper or paper towels. You will find the advantage for this is the ease of cleaning the floor, as well as avoiding it

getting into the drinker. Think how disruptive it will be to clean sawdust up all the time, as opposed to just picking up the paper in sheets. You will probably have to take the soiled sheets out on a daily basis, as you do not want to have a build up of feces, or the keets getting generally messed up.

## 3) FEEDING THE KEETS

### What type of food and water dispensers should you have?

Obviously the brooder will need to be kitted out with suitable feeders, drinkers and of course food and water. It is probably best to buy specific feeders and drinkers for chicks and keets that are effectively mini versions of adult feeders. Again these are readily available from poultry suppliers. The following will cover these aspects more fully. One important safety measure to note about the water dispenser, please ensure that you keep the water as far away from the heat lamp as possible.

### a) Feeding keets

Young keets should in the first few days at least be fed on paper or cardboard to allow them to feed easily. After this, you are well advised to start using a feeding dispenser suitable for chicks. Beyond this, as the keets mature, larger dispensers can be used such as hopper, cylindrical types similar to the ones they will use as adults.

### b) How much food and water should you give the keets?

The keets should never be restricted availability or access to food, as during the initial weeks and months of their lives they are most in need of high protein and are growing at a fast rate. The same is true of fresh daily water.

### c) How often should the keets be fed?

Again, it is advisable to feed the keets ad-lib, that is, as much readily available feed as they can eat. If you prefer to feed them small doses throughout the day, then that is your choice. However be prepared to do this as much as 6 to 8 times in a day.

### d) Introducing the keets to the food and water

The keets usually start to feed within 24 hours, but do not worry if you do not see this straight away as they can comfortably survive for 2 days. Within 48 hours of hatching, the keets will still be benefiting from the yolk that has fed them up until then.

However, it is always a good idea when you first introduce them to the brooder to place the beaks of every keet in the food and water. They will probably find it by themselves anyway, but doing this will obviously make them aware of it sooner. You should then place them under the heat lamp and leave them to it. If you decide to use a tray, or paper for the food, again only do this for the first day or so. The keets will walk in the food and possibly drop feces in it, which of course you should avoid. You certainly do not want to give them water in a shallow tray, for the same reasons, but also there is a risk they could drown.

## Keets drinking water

Water is essential for guinea fowl of all ages but in particular extra care must be given for the keet. Within the first few days, the keet is vulnerable to dehydration, mainly because of exposure to the heat lamp. Water should be available at all times and preferably not be given chilled. The ideal temperature should be about 68° F (20° C). Do not take any chances with the dispenser. The keet needs to be able to get its beak into the drinking part, but should not be able to get in itself as it could drown.

## How far should keets have to travel to water?

The first week in the brooder, the keets will need to be close to the lamp for warmth, but also close enough to the drinker so as not dehydrate. They will need to drink often and so it is recommended to have the drinker as close as 12 inches (30.5cm) to 24 inches (61cm), but not much further than that. To give you some idea of how important the water intake is, they need 3 times the amount of water in comparison to food.

## Keeping the keets safe

Depending on the water dispenser you use, make sure that the part the keets drink out of is not deep enough, that they risk falling in and drowning. If you suspect this, then use small clean gravel or glass marbles in the trough. This should ensure the keets cannot fall in but they can still drink from it. I prefer to use the types of dispenser that has the separate segments going around the trough. The keet will then only be able to get its beak or head in to drink.

## e) What food should the keets be eating?

Chick crumb or turkey starter should be given for the first 6 weeks, then turkey grower from week 6 to week 14. From 14 weeks of age the bird can be fed on turkey breeder or something similar. A lot of keepers strongly advocate ideally feeding them medicated feed initially. Medicated feed is designed to give them the best start. The medication within the feed acts as a preventative measure against certain diseases.

Turkey starter or chick feed is higher in protein than a more standard feed. The extra protein is vital as the keets are growing and developing at a rapid rate. Some of these chick starters are higher in protein than others and some keepers recommend the higher protein and insist that the chicks/keets are larger, stronger and healthier, as a result.

In addition, this should be supplemented with soft, vegetation such as chickweed or lettuce. Avoid hard vegetation such as certain grasses. The keets are not yet able to deal with rough solid food, which an adult would have no problems with, and could lead to an impacted crop.

Until you become experienced, it is probably best that for growing keets age 0 to 12 weeks, that commercial feed mixes are used. These should contain the correct percentage of protein, carbohydrates and all the vitamins and minerals the bird is likely to need. Only very experienced keepers should substitute these for a custom made blend.

Of course as the birds mature towards adulthood, then it is safe to substitute feed for corn and other grains, under normal circumstances. Once the birds enter the breeding season then they will require a specific commercial mix to ensure they receive correct nutrients.

## Medicated feed

As mentioned previously, medicated feed is an advisable starter feed for chicks or keets. As a general rule, you are ideally looking for a medicated feed that will at least combat *coccidiosis*. Amprolium is one such ingredient that you should look out for. This is highly recommended in the initial vulnerable stages of the keets life. You do not need to feed them this forever and can usually stop after a few months.

## Use medicated food sparingly

Please bear in mind that the purpose of any medicated food is to boost the young keet/chick whilst it grows. Some keepers are known to use this for more mature birds to keep them healthy. As you gradually wean the birds off the starter you need to have completed the change over at least 4 weeks before they are at point of lay. You certainly do not want any medication to enter the food chain. If you intended to eat the eggs, you may end up consuming antibiotics and other medications which is most certainly not advisable.

## Keets and protein

As you may expect, in the early stages the young keet is likely to have the potential to grow quicker and faster within a 12 week period. They therefore require a relatively higher level of protein than an adult bird, in those initial stages. The growth process gradually gets less and less as the keets reaches adult size and therefore less and less protein is required. Once growth has peaked and

the bird has reached adulthood, then the growth as such stops. The bird therefore only needs a relatively small percentage of protein to maintain muscle tone and other bodily functions. An increase in protein will also be necessary as the birds go through their seasonal reproduction phase.

## How much protein do keets need?

So, newly hatched keets require the highest percentage of protein for growth and development. Again, chick and turkey starter crumbs are the best and most readily available for this purpose.

Although chick starter is reasonably high in protein, please note, it will not be as high as for example turkey or game bird starter. You are ideally looking for a protein content of around 24 to 26% to start. It doesn't mean that you cannot and must not use chick starter, it just means that they will not develop as well with chick starter as opposed to the other starters.

The recommended protein requirements for keets between the ages of 0 to 4 weeks is said to be between 24 to 26%. After 4 weeks, the protein levels are still important as the keet is still growing and therefore in need of a reasonably high level of protein. However, between the ages of 5 to 8 weeks protein requirements are usually between 17% and 19%. From 4 weeks of age, the keet effectively self regulates intake. In other words the body absorbs as much as it needs and excess protein is unnecessary. However the protein intake is still important, but as the keet grows it requires less. Between the ages of 9 to 12 weeks, protein requirements are around 13% or 14%. By the time the birds reach breeding stage, they require between 14 and 17 % protein.

## Breeder recommended feeding schedule

### 1 month old (growers feed)

Breeders usually recommend to switch from crumbs to 'growers feed' at approximately 1 month old. The protein content is still reasonable at approximately 15%. However you may want to consider supplementing this with chick crumb or turkey starter, as a mix. You would probably do this anyway if you were using a weaning method.

### Weaning and other foods

So, at around the 5 week stage you should ideally be weaning the keets off the high protein *starter* and introducing a *grower* type feed. Depending on your supplier, you may only be able to get a mixed starter/grower variety anyway. There is no need to worry unduly, the birds will still be getting a healthy feed that should at least carry a high enough level of protein.

### Weaning the keets off starter food

As a rough guideline, you can look at spreading the weaning from 5 weeks of age to 10 weeks of age. So for example start the first week (week 5) with a mix that is approximately 5 parts starter 1 part grower. Second week (week 6) make this 4 parts starter and 2 parts grower and so on. At the end of the ninth week, by continuing like this you should have a mix that is 5 parts grower, 1 part starter. So by 10 weeks of age, you should be feeding entirely grower feed, and will hopefully have weaned the keets off the starter altogether. This will

then leave a full 6 week period before the birds have reached 16 weeks and in the case of the hens, are at point of lay.

### What else should the keets be eating?

**Vegetation**

As noted previously, by at least the middle of the second week of birth you should introduce the keets to green vegetation. If you do not have soft grass, chickweed or the like available, then feed shop bought, or your own grown, lettuce.

**Insects**

Towards the end of the second week, you can try them with any available insects.

### Grit for keets

It is also important at this stage to introduce them to grit/oyster shell. You should make grit available, that is suitable for chicks and obviously keets. As with the food, you will probably have to spread this on the floor initially. Then after a week or so you can have this readily available in hoppers.

You need to be specific where the grit is concerned. Adult birds will need much larger grit particles, and the larger particles will be too much for the young growing keets. So even if you have to go to the trouble of purchasing several different sizes, then please do so.

### White millet

One particular seed that the guineas love is white millet. This should not be mistaken with other types of millet, although they will eat other types. For some reason they seem to be very fond of white millet. Many keepers advocate using this as the perfect training aid.

You certainly do not want to spoil them with giving them too much though.

## 4) HEATING THE BROODER

In the section on brooders, we mentioned heating the brooder. We will go into much more detail here about things to watch out for and safety measures.

As you know, if the keets do not have the benefit of a broody hen to keep them warm, then a brooder would be needed. Even with a broody hen, some keepers will advise having a heat lamp in place.

### a) Should the keets need a supplementary heat source?

In general, if you notice the temperature outside has dropped to around 60° F, then it is important that the keets are exposed to a supplementary heat source. Once they are fully feathered and more accustomed to the cold, they should be fine.

### What temperature and humidity do keets need in a brooder?

Brooding keets need a higher temperature than day old chicks. They thrive better at a starting temperature of 90°F (32.2° C) to 95° F (35° C). This is gradually reduced over the next six week so that by six weeks of age, the keets are thriving on a temperature of about 70° F (21.1° C). Some keepers suggest less than this, and generally reduce the temperature in 5° F increments. This reduction by 5° F increments each week takes into account the keets gradually developing feathers and getting used to lower temperatures. Just a note here about the heat lamp: Although the heat lamp will radiate heat generally within the brooder, you should be aware that adjusting the lamp higher or lower, will dictate how hot or cooler it is, directly under the lamp. We will talk more about this shortly.

Ideally a humidity of around 65 and 70% should be maintained, but can be difficult in certain cold, dry climates. The water dispenser will probably be the main source of atmospheric moisture. This again is another important reason to ensure that water dispensers are kept as full as possible and never allowed to dry out. Humidity is also important where dust can be a problem and the moist air helps keep this down. Once again, dry air and dust can cause all manor of respiratory problems.

### b) Heating source in the brooder

Unlike a relatively sealed incubator, you will have difficulty keeping a constant heat throughout the brooder. Many keepers recommend the use of a 60 to 100 watt bulb as a heat source. At first you should suspend the light about 12 inches to 18 inches (30 cm to 45 cm approx) above the floor. Some keepers will advocate using this and not necessarily adjusting it. This should be fine providing the keets can stand under the lamp with no risk of the bulb touching their head and burning it. In this way you find that the keets will either stand under the light as they need the extra warmth, or move away to cool off.

### Do you need a special heat lamp?

Specific heat lamps that you can buy from livestock and poultry suppliers, usually come with an aluminum or other metal hood. If you can get something similar from a DIY store, then by all means use that. If not, then buy from a supplier. They are far more efficient than a bulb without as they radiate a localized heat source. Where ever you fix this, be sure that the cable and light is securely fixed. You do not want this to drop to the floor and either injure a keet or create a fire risk.

### c) Suggested temperatures to use for the heat lamp

There are various suggestion for the correct lamp or spot temperature and these generally range from 36° C to 38° C on day one to 20° C to 22° C by week 5.

» So an average temperature for the first two days would be 98.6° F (37° C).

» From day 3 to day 7 the average is 95° F (35°C).

» Day 7 to day 14, 89.6° F (32° C).

» Day 14 to day 21, 82.4° F (28° C).

» Day 21 to day 28, 77° F (25° C).

» Day 28 to day 35, 69.8° F (21° C)

By the end of week 6 they should be fully feathered and therefore able to generate and retain body heat, greater than from week one.

So how do you ensure that the keets are getting these temperatures? Well as previously mentioned, we are talking about the heat radiating directly under the lamp. What you would therefore need to do is, once the lamp is hung, take a thermometer and take the temperature approximately where the top of the keets head would be. If the temperature is lower than recommended you would have to lower the lamp. Conversely, if this is too high then you would have to raise the lamp. If you lower the lamp and it is still not generating enough heat, you will probably have to use a stronger bulb.

### d) Installing the heat lamp

It is also important that you have the heat source at one end of the sleeping section. By having the heat source at one end, the keets can move away to the cooler part at the other end. Be aware that the light-bulb should not be too close to any wall, as this could create a fire risk. You should then be able to adjust the height of this so that it is close enough to the keets to provide sufficient heat and not to close to any object liable to become a fire risk. This should be above the head height of the keets but not too far away that you struggle to feel the benefit, about 6" (15.2 cm), should suffice.

## Health and safety

Wherever heaters or heat lamps are placed you should always ensure they are in the safest location, i.e. close enough for it to be effective, but not too close to cause a potential fire hazard. Heat lamps in particular should never be too low that there is a risk of burning the keets.

## e) Behavior to look out for in the brooder

1. You can use the following as indicators as to whether the keets are too hot or cold. There are generally 4 indicators that you should look out for when observing the keets under a heat lamp.

2. **Ideal temperature:** The keets appear generally happy, unstressed and untroubled. Most noticeably they should be generally spread out under the heat lamp. The lamp is at the correct height and the keets are getting as much heat as they need.

3. **The temperature is too low.** In this case the keets will be huddled in a cluster. They are obviously needing extra warmth as they are directly below the lamp and are huddled to conserve and generate heat. The lamp is too high and so the spot temperature is not enough for what they need. You need to lower the lamp, so that they receive more heat.

4. **The temperature is too high**: The keets remain on the outskirts of the lamp, in other words, they avoid being directly underneath the lamp. They may show signs of overheating such as panting and showing general signs of heat exhaustion. In direct opposition to the lamp being to high, in this case the lamp is too low and needs to be raised.

5. If you notice the keets are all congregating to one side of the lamp, then the following could be the problem. This fourth point may occur if there is something bothering the keets on one side of the lamp. It could be mainly due to a draught blowing down one side of the lamp and they are obviously trying to avoid this. It could be that the light is too bright or something else disturbing them on the opposite side of where they are gathered. You will need to investigate further, check for draughts etc, and attempt to put this right.

### *Keets fully feathered*

Once the birds reach full adult hood, they will be fully feathered and hardened. Despite guinea fowl originating from the warm climes of the Southern Hemisphere, they have adapted and cope surprisingly well in extreme Northern Hemisphere temperatures. It is not unusual for adult birds to roost in trees overnight in temperatures as low as -23° C (-10° F)

### *Monitoring the behavior of the keets*

Remember, you should keep an eye on how the keets are doing. If you notice them huddling together they are likely to be too cold. If they seem to be spread about and avoiding the lamp, they are probably too hot. In both cases either raise or lower the lamp. If it is still too hot, then you may need to add extra ventilation to the inside by leaving a gap in the lid.

### *e) What if you have 2 separate clutches of keets?*

You may sometimes decide to hatch two separate batches of eggs, perhaps a few days apart. You should be able to introduce the new keets into an existing brooder without any real problem. What you should be aware of though, is that the youngest keets will require more heat than the older ones. It is therefore recommended that you set the heat as previously mentioned for newly introduced keets. You may experience some, pecking from the older keets, but this shouldn't last, as they get used to the new arrivals. The younger keets will naturally be intimidated initially, but they will soon settle in.

If you had a broody hen with keets and incubated eggs that were hatching roughly the same time, you may be tempted to introduce some keets and therefore mix them. This can be done relatively easy within the first few days, but should not be attempted much after this. The newly hatched keets could be attacked or rejected. It is therefore safer if in doubt to make alternative arrangements. In this case with a separate pen and brooder.

## 5) ADDITIONAL BROODER INFORMATION

### *Brooder On a daily basis*

As before you should monitor daily food and water supply, and regularly clean out any damp or dirt, replenishing with fresh bedding. You do not want to risk your baby keets picking up an infection, so hygiene is particularly important at this stage.

### *Problems with shavings and sawdust*

Shavings or sawdust is also not a good idea for the keets in the initial stages as there is a risk they may eat this. Wood from saw mills can be treated and the chemical could easily affect the keets. As the birds get older, they are unlikely to attempt to eat this anyway.

### *Ventilation*

Ventilation is important at any stage of the birds life as they need fresh intakes of oxygen and the expulsion of carbon dioxide. However it is suggested that keeping ventilation to a minimum will ensure that relative humidity is retained in the brooder. As most brooders have an external, non heated part anyway, they will get sufficient fresh, non stuffy air anyway. However, it is equally important that the ventilation does not create a draught. A draught can soon create a chill in the air. Until the keets develop feathers and therefore have the ability to generate and retain their own body heat, they are relying on outside heat sources, i.e. from a lamp or broody hen.

## Outside of the brooder

As the keets mature, you may wish to allow the hen and keets outside of the brooder for extra fresh air etc. Small move-able coops with runs can make very good outside brooders for a hen and keets to take advantage of fresh air and vegetation. If you have a large grass area, these can be moved about on a daily basis. You need to ensure these are brought inside on a night in case of predator attacks. These can be moved, over a fresh piece of grass/ground on a daily basis. Ensure that these are strong enough to withstand a dog trying to break in during the day, and particularly if you leave them during the day.

## Introducing a perch

As you notice the keets becoming stronger and jumping about, you can introduce a perch at one end of run. Use either a suitable branch or 1" x 1" (2.5 cm x 2.5 cm) timber with the edges rounded. This does not want to be too high off the ground. So something that is 2 or 3 inches (5.1cm or 7.6 cm) off the floor, should not cause any injuries if they happen to fall off.

## Cleaning

Once you have finished with the brooder it is always a good idea to clean and disinfect it for future use. Any bacteria that may be in the brooder will not therefore have a chance to develop.

# CHAPTER TEN

# RAISING THE KEETS

In this chapter we will look at the keets as they develop from hatch-lings to adults.

## 1) OVERVIEW OF REARING THE KEETS

signs of a keet with head drooping looking ill etc, then you should isolate the

Once the keets begin to hatch, the first week will be crucial for their survival. Guinea fowl are hardy creatures and purists will insist that they survive in the wild without special treatment. However, care must be taken as keets can and do die. But if you follow the basic guidelines given here and the previous chapter, you will give them the best chance.

Within the first week keets could die from dehydration, failure to eat, becoming chilled or too hot, injuring themselves, drowning in a drinking receptacle that they manage to get into.

### *Watching keets for signs of illness*

Once the keets are past the first critical 7 days then they will be getting stronger and more able. If you see any

bird to a hospital area. This can be an animal carrier or a box you make yourself. It should obviously be clean and disinfected. Have a heat source as well as fresh clean shaving/sawdust litter. Of course fresh water and food should be available. Once the bird is isolated then it should pose no further risk to other birds. You should seek veterinary advice in order to establish what the bird may be suffering from. This should not be ignored as it could be something that potentially affects the whole flock.

### *Venturing outside*

After several days, up to a week of feeding and watering the keets inside the enclosed brooder, you can try them outside. After that time, it will be safe to introduce them to a larger area, sometimes referred to as a nursery. This will allow them more freedom to move about and explore. By this I don't mean the big wide open hen house, or the free range part, but the run part that you hopefully have as part of the internal brooder. This is to encourage them into the outside part more, so that they are mainly coming indoors if they are chilled. It is still a good idea to provide an internal brooding area that the keets can escape to if they need extra warmth.

## 2) HOW LONG SHOULD THE KEETS BE IN THE BROODER?

The brooder/run combination, that we have previously talked about, should be adequate accommodation for the first six weeks. Remember that at the end of each week you should be aiming to reduce the heat.

There seems to be much debate as to the length of time keets should remain in the brooder. Some keepers will tell you 6 weeks, others will insist they only need to stay for 7 days. It is perhaps best to look at keeping them there for a minimum 14 days. There is no prize for how quickly you can release them, so at least give them a reasonable time while they are at their most vulnerable.

A lot depends on the weather at the time, although it is unlikely you will be raising them in October/November time. It also depends where they are transferred to once they leave the brooder. As mentioned previously, the gradual reduction in heat source is intended to harden them so eventually they have no heat to rely on. You can gauge this by checking the current temperature inside the brooder and adjust accordingly.

You will be able to judge whether they are comfortable with a higher or lower heat. You certainly do not want to switch the heat off all together as they are still likely to need heat. If you notice they spend most of their time in the outside pen area, then you can perhaps switch the heat off during the day, but leave it on overnight, when the temperature drops anyway.

### Keeping the keets dry

Make sure the keets stay warm and dry for at least the first 4 weeks. Should they become wet or become damp they can soon chill and possibly die.

### What if some of the keets die?

Within the first week you may experience one or two keets that unfortunately die. This could be no more than a congenital condition, and there is probably not a great deal you could have done to prevent it. Providing you have supplied a safe clean environment with food and water, you can do no more. The keets quickly develop and gain strength in a matter of days. You certainly need to keep them warm and dry at this stage as they are still vulnerable to diseases such as coccidiosis.

### Why do the keets need an outdoor space?

Once again, the idea of the outdoor space is that if the inside becomes too warm they can escape to a cooler part. It also serves to acclimatize the keets to the normal outdoor temperature. With this in mind, your run, external brooder part is likely to be a basic frame covered with chicken wire. In the initial stages however, you may need to put boards up around and on top of the run to prevent

any drafts.

### Keets at week 8

If the keets are not to be introduced to other adult birds you may have such as chickens, you can allow them the freedom of the main hen house when they get to about 8 weeks of age. This will have high perches in place that the keets will be more than capable of flying up to.

It is best to gradually introduce the keets like this as they are less likely to get injured attempting to fly up to high perches.

If you do have other poultry in the main hen house, you are advised to keep the keets in the safe nursery area until they are about 12 weeks old. By this time they will not be too traumatized by the inevitable pecking order that is likely to take place. With that in mind it is always advisable that with the exception of the period in the incubation area, they should have full view of the hen house. In that respect, these new arrivals will not be strangers to the other inhabitants.

### The keets first venture into the main hen house

Your guinea keets will have been in the segregated brooder/nursery area, ideally for approximately six weeks. They should now be ready to release in with the other mature birds. Although they will have been able to see the activity of the hen house whilst in the brooder, it will be very strange to wander out into the hen house itself. It is advisable at this point, to not have the older birds in the hen house. So as you let the older birds out into the outside run, make sure they all go out and then shut the door. You can then open the door of the brooder into the hen house and let the keets come out and explore. You should allow them a good few hours to do this and if you have time, stay with them and observe.

## 3) Mixing keets with older birds

Once you finally decide to allow the keets access to the main coop, along with the other adult birds, I would advise the following for an easy transition. The brooder door into the hen house should be left open in case the keets decide to retreat should they become frightened. This entrance also needs to be only big enough for the keets to enter and not an adult bird. You will no doubt notice the older birds take a peck or chase the keets. This is only natural as the older birds wish to establish a pecking order. This should soon calm down when they all become familiar with each other.

### When do you let the keets out into the outside pen?

Please be aware that everything discussed so far has been in relation to the keets been in the brooder then allowed into the hen house/coop. At some point the transition needs to take place from coop to outside run and consequently, free range.

Keepers of guinea fowl have different ideas about keeping the keets confined to the chicken coop, before letting them into the outside run. Some insist that they should be kept in the hen house for the first 6 weeks or so, so that this gets imprinted on them. They then let them out into the outside pen for their first taste of being free range. At first they may be wary of stepping out into the unknown. Some will be braver than others and wander out, for the others to then follow. Do not rush them at this stage, as their natural curiosity will

eventually take them all outside.

### Releasing the keets into an open topped run

If the main enclosure does not have an open roof then it doesn't matter what time of day you do this. However, if they run free range, you would be advised to release them first thing in the morning. If any manage to fly over the fence, then they have the whole day to find their way back. What you do not want, is to release them late afternoon or evening. If one or two do fly over and wander off, they may become disoriented and may not be able to make it back. It would be a big risk at this stage, as they would be easy prey for a predator.

The young keets will certainly have been trained to recognize the hen house as home, and where their food comes from at this stage. They will therefore hopefully not want to wander very far if, at all.

### Free range; releasing keets into the open

Again, if you release the keets into an open free range area, they will probably not travel too far. They will certainly be on their guard for anything strange and soon move out of the way of danger. In the evening, when the light starts to fade, they will soon get used to returning to the hen house to roost. Any stragglers should be encouraged back into the hen house. At first, if you have trouble getting them to realize they have to come back to the hen house to roost, start to train them with a favorite treat such as white millet. Training will be covered later, but once they get used to this treat, it doesn't take a great deal of training to get them to come to you. If you call to them, they will soon know that this means they should return home and they will get a treat.

### What to feed keets when you have poultry other than guinea fowl?

We have already covered feeding previously, but this takes into account mixing with adult birds. By the time you release your new Guinea keets with the adult birds they will be able to fend for themselves. If you have mixed poultry already, then there is no need to feed the guineas anything other than what you already feed the other birds. If these are your first and only birds then there are a number of suitable feeds available. If for example the birds were in their laying season, a breeder/layer type food would be advisable. This contains more protein than a standard feed. When the birds have stopped laying towards winter time then you only need to feed a lower protein mix, to give them the necessary sustenance.

### Changes taking place as the keet grows

The fluffy covering the keets have, gradually disappears as the weeks go by. By 12 weeks of age the keets will be looking more like adult Guinea Fowl and should be showing the start of the bony helmet protrusion and a head and neck that is going bald.

You may also see keets of the same age at different sizes of growth. Some grow quickly, others take time and appear stunted then they all of a sudden grow to the size of the others in a short space of time.

### Socializing keets

Guinea Fowl at any age can easily panic. If the birds have been socialized, imprinted or whatever, then they will be used to human contact. Failure to do this will result in the birds naturally resorting to their wild tendencies. Large groups of birds will flock and crowd together if panicked, and cause some to get injured or at worse crushed.

### Humanizing; handling the keets

Socializing by handling the keets should occur as soon as possible and preferably on a daily basis. A key point in behavioral training is to handle the keets as young as possible. By handling the keets as regularly as possible, you will socialize them to the extent that this should reduce any wild tendencies. You will know within the first week if you should handle them more. They will soon become very familiar with you and show no fear by running away. The longer you leave it to handle them, the harder it will be to build their trust and confidence in human contact.

By this point your keets should be fully transitioned adults, if not getting there. You will now have done all you can to raise your keets from birth to adult hood.

# CHAPTER ELEVEN

# GUINEA FOWL HEALTH

We will cover here the health of your Guinea Fowl, as well as potential diseases and ailments that could affect them at some point.

# 1) CHECKING THE HEALTH OF THE FLOCK

As a matter of routine you should check how your birds are doing. You will notice straight away if a bird is ill and listless. You should consequently investigate further, as a disease could affect the rest of the flock.

Any birds that you suspect may be ill should be handled to see if there is any loss of muscle definition. If they are not old, they may have a condition or disease that may require the expert opinion of the vet.

## A) FIRST AID

A basic first aid kit for your birds would be a good idea. Unless you have a bird unfortunate to break a limb and require a splint and bandages, only a few medicines will be necessary.

For wounds and general infections an often recommended product is Vetericyn VF (veterinary formula). This is a general purpose spray to use on wounds, abrasions, skin ulcers, fungal infections, eye and ear infections, rashes etc. It purports to contain a compound that is similar to chemicals produced naturally by an animals own immune system response. It is a non toxic, antibiotic free solution, that is suitable for a whole host of animals including dogs, horses and of course poultry.

Anything else can be bought as and when you need them. As a preventative measure you may wish to have some sort of dusting powder to apply to dust bathing areas.

## What to do if you suspect a bird of having an illness or injury?

Any birds that you notice showing symptoms of an illness or an injury should be isolated as soon as possible. Injured birds will no doubt receive hostility from the other birds. A sick bird needs to be isolated for the same reason, but also to eliminate the risk of a contagious disease spreading.

## Having an isolation pen/sick bay

For sick or injured birds you are strongly advised to have an isolation area. If you do not have a suitable pen, then it is always a good idea to have a large pet cage/crate (*you can use a search term in Google such as* [dog cage/crate for sale] *for example*), on hand. Unless the bird has a contagious disease, if at all possible it is advisable that the pen is within sight of the rest of the flock. Once you separate a bird from the flock, even for a couple of days, you can experience all manner of attacks from the other birds on its return.

## Animal hospital

You can also purchase plastic animal carriers that also make an excellent substitute hospital area for a sick or injured bird. Attachable food and water dishes can also be used, to prevent spillages on the floor. In their isolation area they can cohabit with the other birds, but in the safety of the cage where no other bird can bully or attack them.

You should line the cage or area with a good few inches of soft bedding material. They may well need a source of heat as well as water, food and any medicated water that may be needed for the sick bird.

What should you do if you find a dead bird or birds?

Sometimes it is an unfortunate consequence that when you have livestock you also get dead stock. In most disease cases that you do not have experience of, it may be wise to contact a vet for medical advice. If you suspect any disorder is not serious, and you seem certain that the condition, perhaps worms can be treated easily, then you can buy such treatments over the counter at pet stores and general animal suppliers. Professional advice should always be sought on more serious matters. Some diseases can affect whole flocks, and the last thing you want is to have all of your flock suffering. This is why it is important to isolate a suspected bird before things get out of hand.

### Facing having a bird put down

It is always hard to raise any animal as a pet and have to face having the poor thing put down. Sometimes this can be inevitable, and in some cases the bird would only suffer any way. You may also receive bad news from a vet that they can try certain treatment but there are no guarantees and it is likely to cost a lot of money. The choice of what you do is yours, but sometimes it is understandable if you decide to have the unfortunate bird put to sleep.

### B) SHOULD YOU CONTACT A VETERINARIAN?

It is not easy to advise as to whether or when you should contact a veterinarian. As you gain experience you will learn that there is a lot that you can self diagnose and treat. We will cover a lot of common health issues shortly.

Forums are another excellent place that often have searches for specific conditions you may be worried about. There are also a wealth of enthusiasts that will be only too happy to answer a specific question, once you join.

As far as contacting a vet, I would always recommend you do this if you are uncertain about a condition or disease one or all of your birds has. Particularly if you suspect it may be serious.

The main problem with calling the vet for the slightest thing is the cost factor. Vets are experts, but as a result of this, are costly. Some people will never take a sick animal to the vet no matter what, and some will take them for everything. Some will take them only if they suspect a serious problem.

You do of course have peace of mind by getting an expert diagnosis. However, until you have this knowledge, it is probably best to consult with a veterinarian. Again, ultimately the choice is yours.

### C) NEW BIRDS INTRODUCING PARASITES AND DISEASE

Sometimes as a keeper you may wish to add to your flock, or someone offers you several birds free. A disadvantage of introducing new birds to the flock is potential parasites or diseases that the new birds may be carrying. This could be a difficult one because without doing a series of expensive laboratory tests you are not likely to know for sure. You should at least consider keeping the new birds in quarantine so you can check for external parasites.

### D) LEG PROBLEMS WITH GUINEA FOWL

Guinea Fowl can be prone to limping. If you suspect a sprain and not a break, this will no doubt heal itself after a week or so. You should be particularly careful where keets are concerned. Accidents do happen and occasionally they will fly or jump onto something, slide off and cause themselves an injury. Sometimes they may slip on a wet surface, or misjudge flying up-to a perch or tree stump, and fall off.

### Leg problems what should you do?

In most cases there is not a great deal you can do. But if there is anything in the hen house or the run that looks as if it is an accident waiting to happen then try and remove this or put something in place to deter them. Quite often feed hoppers strung from the ceiling, seem to be appealing places to roost. Apart from the fact that they may drop feces into the feed, they could get a leg tangled in the chain or rope holding it up. Anything such as that, needs to have some sort of a barrier or shield attached to prevent possible injuries. Sometimes these things are not so obvious until an accident happens and you simply have to put it down to experience.

### What if you come across adult birds with deformities?

Deformities in birds can be a sign that the birds are inbred, ie the product of a close relation. In this case it is necessary to rotate the stock from time to time, with new blood. If you have started the keets off with good quality starter, this will no doubt contain all the vitamins and minerals necessary for correct development.

### E) Land disease/Sour ground

Although land is mentioned elsewhere, as part of accommodating the Guinea Fowl, it is briefly discussed here in relation to possible diseases. Land may be used, either several acres of free range, or a much smaller run that most keepers are likely to encounter. You are only likely to encounter problems with land disease if it is over-crowded and therefore over-used. Sour ground and diseases that will potentially affect productivity are caused because feces have been allowed to build up, and the ground isn't given chance to repair itself. It is therefore important that you consider the recommended space requirement for each bird.

If sour ground becomes a problem, grass will soon disappear. In most cases the grass does not have chance to grow back. Grass can also disappear if over-grazed. In drier areas, particularly during the summer months, grass can soon dry out. If you notice this and dry mud patches appear that do not seem to be replenished then and irrigation system may be required.

### Possible diseases from free range sour ground.

Free range birds can be at risk of coccidiosis and other diseases as well as worms. If there is an over abundance of feces, that is either infected or becomes infected, then as birds feed, they could easily pick up these diseases.

It is estimated that each bird will produce approximately 75kg (165 pound approx) to 95 kg (210 pound approx) of feces per year.

According to one estimated source at the following:

http://www.soils.wisc.edu/extension/pubs/A3392.pdf

it is estimated that no more 25 tons of solid dairy manure or the equivalent phosphorus level, should be spread on one acre in one year. However, it is a well known fact that poultry manure has a higher nitrogen and phosphate content than most manures. On page 5 of the above document, the equivalent given for poultry manure is 5 tons per acre recommended per year.

So as an example 5 metric tons is 5000 kilograms. Therefore 5000 kg divided by 95 kg would be equal to 52.6. so according to that information approximately 53 birds will produce the recommended safe amount of manure for 1 acre of land. If you have free range birds, you can obviously see that more than 53 birds per acre, according to these findings, is likely to cause you problems with sour land.

I do not wish to get into the whole scientific facts and statistics covering this subject. However, I have known free range keepers that accommodate 100 birds plus on an acre of land, without any devastating effects. It could well be, that the land in question was of a poor quality with very little nitrogen and phosphate content to start with. Over time a high build up and perhaps 'overdose' could well cause problems. What does seem clear is that poultry manure is high in nitrogen and phosphate, in comparison to other manures. It should therefore be used sparingly.

You can therefore see that the over-stocking of land, however big can cause devastating effects. It may be possible to rotate land use, i.e. use a piece of land for part of the year, move the stock, and leave it fallow. This would give the land time to make use of any manure build up. But if land is used in this manner then it may be more feasible to use the same land all the time, with the correct number of birds. If you use a rotation system, you have to stock an acre with 200 to 300 birds for example, and then move them and leave the acre fallow. In other words you will need 2 acres to make it work, so you may as well stock 50 to 150 birds on the one acre.

## 2) DEFICIENCY DISEASES

The following, as the title suggests, are diseases that have been known to affect Guinea Fowl, as a result of a deficiency of some sort. They are not placed in any particular order of importance. Many are included for reference and historical purposes and you may find that non of them ever affect your Guinea Fowl.

### a) Crazy chick disease (encephalomalacia)

This is usually caused by a lack of vitamin E in the young keet. If manifests as a lack of control in the muscles, that makes eating and walking difficult. Prevention is the best solution and simply involves a diet with recommended vitamin E given to the hen during the egg laying phase. Layers feed given to hens is likely to provide enough vitamin E.

### b) Curly toe disease

Paralysis of the toe or **curly toe disease** is usually due to a lack of vitamin B2. Again the correct commercial feed mix should contain sufficient vitamin content to not make this a problem. Alternative sources of vitamin B2 are riboflavin, dried yeast and skimmed milk.

### c) Rickets (osteomalacia)

Rickets is caused by another vitamin deficiency, this time vitamin D3. It causes a phosphorus/calcium imbalance deformed bones in the leg and rib cage. The bones of older birds can fracture and this isn't due to the bones becoming brittle, but actually softer and weaker. This is something the keeper of Guinea Fowl needs to be aware of because the Guinea Fowl needs more of this vitamin than other poultry.

### d) Sinusitis

As you may expect this affects the cavities of the head and in Guinea Fowl can be either infected cavities or a vitamin A deficiency. These cavities and nasal passages can become affected by dust or grain particle etc being lodged there in some way. It generally results in a nasal discharge and the bird can often be seen shaking its head as if trying to alleviate the problem. You should check, by inspecting the nasal passage, that there is no such foreign body, lodged there. You may need a torch or other strong light to properly see. It may also be necessary to check with a vet in the first instance, in case this is a vitamin A problem or some other infection.

### e) Feather picking

This is generally considered to be a behavioral problem associated with cramped conditions, excessive light, boredom, aggression and are all associated with stress. It can also be as a result of a lack of protein or some other element that is lacking in the birds diet. This is more likely to happen to large producers or birds in battery cages, but again can be a symptom of overcrowding. Beak trimming is often seen as a solution, but should only ideally be considered as a last resort. The birds as part of their health routine, should be allowed to preen their feathers and beak clipping

is likely to inhibit this. Any birds that persistently cause problems should be isolated from the flock. In the same way the victim will need isolating to prevent repeat attacks from other birds and of course to recover.

### f) Botulism

This is caused by a bacteria known as *clostridial.* The disease is often referred to as limp or limber neck, because of it affecting the neck muscles and causing it partial paralysis or to hang limp. This is a condition that results from an unhygienic environment, and can obviously be remedied by keeping everywhere regularly cleaned and disinfected. Professional advice should be sought should this become a regular problem or it occurs despite your impeccable hygiene standards. Culling is often recommended in birds that are affected.

### g) Bumblefoot

A wound or injury can sometimes result in an infection known as *staphylococcus.* The sole of the foot can become swollen which can often be as the result of an abscess. The usual remedy for this is to lance and clean the affected area with antiseptic solution and finally, treat with antibiotics. If you are experienced with this procedure then you may choose to do this yourself. However, if you are in any doubt please seek professional advice.

### h) Favus

This is a fungal infection that manifests itself as scabs whitish or grey in color. This can appear around the cloaca and other exposed areas of the body. This is an externally treated condition, i.e. an anti fungal solution can be applied. However, this can be a symptom of an underlying problem such as a congenital weakness or over use of antibiotics.

## 3) OTHER PROBLEMATIC CONDITIONS

### a) Impacted crop

This can affect keets if they eat fibrous grass that they cannot manage at that young age. Adult birds can pick up similar indigestible objects such as string or plastic. The crop itself will feel solid and obviously larger than normal. Apart from this the bird will usually not wish to eat and may seem listless.

There are a number of remedies that include poring a suitable liquid down the birds throat. This can be a warm water and oil mix that you then massage, whilst holding the bird in an inverted position. The idea for inverting the bird is that it drains both the fluid and the obstruction.

Sometimes if the impaction is particularly bad, it may be necessary to open the crop up surgically. This is not a procedure I would advise anyone to tackle and it is certainly not advisable for an inexperienced beginner.

### b) Sour crop

Again the crop is swollen, however the contents are usually more liquid. You approach this in a similar way as above by holding the affected bird so its head points to the ground. You should always hold the bird around the body. Be sure not to hold the bird by the legs, as Guinea Fowl in particular do not have as strong legs as say a chicken. Once again you massage the crop until the liquid

comes out of the birds mouth. An old remedy to dose the bird after this is to dissolve a pinch of bicarbonate of soda in warm water. You can pour this or use a syringe to administer the solution down the birds throat. If you suspect that the case may be more serious, then as always seek the advice of a veterinarian.

### c) What if the keet has deformed limbs?

Deformed feet or limbs could well have happened inside the egg as the bird was growing. Splayed legs or crooked limbs can be remedied when the keet is young. You simply tape or bind these, with a splint if necessary. In the case of splayed legs, you can use string tied to one leg and you draw the other leg into a normal position so both feet are straight upright under the birds body. Some people use rubber bands as these are quite sturdy but flexible.

## 4) GUINEA FOWL PARASITES

It is perhaps obvious to state that birds having exposure to free range land rather than a controlled commercial unit, will be more susceptible to parasite infestation. As the free range bird picks about for food they can easily pick up worms or infected feces from wild birds or rodents. Birds in controlled units however, are generally only fed commercially available feed and pumped water. Although poultry infested with parasites rarely die from the actual parasite, death can be caused by secondary infection due to attacks on internal organs. In general, symptoms of a parasite infestation can include a general loss of condition; reduced production of eggs; keets that seem slow to develop and dull damaged feathers.

The parasite will typically rob the host of natural resources. Blood loss; the parasite is taking nutrition from the food resources that the birds needs to survive and for optimum health. The body is using up energy in repairing lesion damage etc, caused by the parasite. The immune system is compromised as the body tries to fight infection.

### a) Internal Parasites

Worms are the main internal parasite likely to affect the Guinea Fowl. With an infestation of worms, the bird is likely to appear lethargic and generally lacking in health. The parasite is usually passed on through any possible infected means. This could be infected feces, food, or otherwise. In this respect as with a lot of other diseases, rigorous health management is a must. So regular cleaning and disinfecting; ensuring food does not become sour or stale; clean, dry litter or bedding; clean food and water dispensers, with fresh clean water.

It may be necessary to get a proper diagnosis of which type of worm is affecting the bird.

The following is an overview of the most common parasitic worms known to affect Guinea Fowl:

### b) Roundworms (ascaris galli)

These can affect both adult and keet and are usually present in the small intestine. They can be as long as 7 or 8 cm (2 ¾ inch or just over 3 inch), and are white in color. Self diagnosis can occur if you happen to see one in the feces which can sometimes happen. Otherwise you may have to contact a professional for an accurate diagnosis. It is usually caused by litter/bedding that is damp. Once diagnosis is established the birds can be easily dosed, usually with an additive to the drinking water.

### c)Ascaridiasis: (Ascaridia) (A numidae)
### A numidae (roundworm)
### H gallinarum (pin worm)

The adult *ascaridia* parasite lives in the small intestine of the host. However the larvae of the parasite, affects the outer mucous membranes of the mouth, eyes, nostrils, cloaca etc. *A numidae* (roundworm), affects both chickens and Guinea Fowl. It has been found in Africa, Europe, South America and parts of the USA.

Symptoms can include; thirst, weakness, weight loss, restricted growth in young birds.

Professional fecal analysis will confirm its presence and consequent recommended treatment.

### d) Pin worms (heterakis gallinae)

These are only about 1 cm (½ inch approx), long and are quite thin, like a pin or a hair. They cause little problem to the bird and are usually easily treated.

### e) Hairworm, threadworm, crop worm: (capillariasis; capillaria spp)

These are tiny hair like parasites that live in the intestine of the host.

Symptoms of an infestation include: listlessness, vomiting, weight loss, thickening of the crop and oesophagus.

Detection is by feces and mucous sampling. Once again professional diagnosis and advice on treatment should be sought.

## f) Thread worms (capillaria contorta)

These can be problematic for keets as well as adults. It usually affects older keets of up to 8 weeks old and they can show a lack of appetite, appearing generally ill. They also tend to shiver which at first may appear as if they are cold. They can become very thirsty and a yellow liquid diarrhea emitted. They also become quite thin and within a few days die.

Adults also emit diarrhea and again they become thin, but their deterioration is over a matter of weeks.

Once again a correct diagnosis should be sought from a professional.

## g) Gape worms (syngamus trachea)

These are up to 2 cm (¾ inch approx) long. They are parasitic blood suckers and as a result are colored red. They are difficult to shift as they attach themselves to the walls of the trachea. If you have birds with skin parasites, you should check that these are not present also. They often appear at the same time as skin parasites.

As these affect the trachea it is perhaps unsurprisingly that affected birds are seen coughing and wheezing.

This parasite is present worldwide and is usually contracted via intermediary hosts such as earthworm, slugs and snails. Once ingested the gapeworm travels to the lungs and trachea, thus affecting the birds ability to breathe, hence gape or gasping for breath. On free range, if an infestation has taken place, it is often necessary to move the flock and to leave the land fallow. As there is likely to be a residual presence of the worms and eggs, ploughing and treating the soil is often required. It may also be necessary to restrict younger birds as they are thought to be more at risk than older birds.

The condition is treatable but symptoms of coughing can exist for a while as the bird attempt to expel dead or dying worms.

## h) Gizzard worms (acuaria hamulosa)

They are up to 2 cm (¾ inch approx) long and is a red/brown color. These worms are thought to be transmitted by grasshoppers. Affected birds will show weight loss and obvious problems with digestion as the gizzard is an important part of the process. Seek veterinarian advice.

## i) Tape worms (davainea proglottina)

Tape worm sections are often seen in feces as they periodically break off from the main worm. They can be over 20 cm (8 inch approx) in length and have a distinctive flat sectional form. The head itself is usually firmly attached to the intestinal wall by a network of hooks. As with other parasites that feed off the bird it will not be surprising if the affected bird becomes thin. This is not as serious as some of the worms and parasites but should be eradicated as soon as possible once diagnosis is made. Again seek advice and recommended treatment from a vet.

## j) Flukes: (trematodes)

They can be transmitted to poultry via dragonfly, snails, contact with wild birds or ponds and mollusc's.

## 5) ECTOPARASITES, (EXTERNAL PARASITES)

Older buildings can be a particular problem with external parasites. They typically thrive in a dirty, dusty, damp and dark environment. As a routine you should endeavor to carry out a thorough cleanse and disinfect every 6 months and no later than once per year. This is provided there is no immediate problem. If the problem is immediate then it will be necessary to do this immediately and repeat the process several times over a few weeks or month.

The following are common external parasites that could potentially affect Guinea Fowl

### a) Fowl tick (argas persicus)

These parasites are nocturnal blood suckers and are carriers of a bacteria known as *leptospiral*, which causes *spirochaetosis*. There are a number of other varieties of tick that exist in Australia and the Americas. As well as treating the bird, it is usually necessary to treat the living quarters as they can live in cracks and crevices. Insecticidal treatments such as Permethrin are usually administered, but if in any doubt consult with a vet for accurate diagnosis.

Blood is needed in the ticks reproduction phase, to produce eggs. But when not reproducing, adults can survive without the blood feed for a year or more. Like mites they live off the host in cracks and crevices. Unlike mites they usually feed in less than 1 hour in some cases only 30 minutes.

Notable symptoms are weight loss and anemia as a result of blood loss. They are also known to transmit certain diseases such as fowl cholera and lyme disease.

### b) Bugs (cimicidae)

Commonly known as bed bugs in an infested household. Again these tend to be nocturnal and feed on the blood of the birds. They are about ½ cm (¼ inch) long, and have brownish wide flat bodies. An appropriate insecticidal treatment such as Ivermectin, should be used to eradicate the infestation.

### c) Lice

Lice seem to be the most prolific parasites affecting Guinea Fowl. Unlike the blood sucking parasites, they feed on skin and feathers. There are usually 3 types that affect either the head, body or the shaft of the feather. They are usually less than 4mm (0.4cm) in length. Head lice are a light grey color. Body and feather shaft lice are a yellow color. You tend to find what appear to be clusters on the shaft of feathers or the skin itself. Dusting powders or a lotion such as Ivermectin, are the usual treatment for lice. When using dusting powders, it is also recommended to treat the bedding and dusting areas as well as the birds.

### d) Lice: (phthiraptera)

Generally cause irritation to the skin and so the birds will be irritable, scratching and preening. It can even cause sleep loss. They are easily detectable by carefully ruffling the feathers, and can easily be seen with the naked eye.

They are easily treatable with a number of chemical solutions and dusting powders.

## e) Mites

As these are difficult to see without at least a magnifying glass, obvious signs of these are; the birds will become irritable and scratch and pull at the feathers. The skin usually has red scaly patches. The following are the most common affecting Guinea Fowl and other poultry. Dusting powders or broad spectrum anti-parasitic formulas such as Ivermectin, are generally administered.

## f) Quill and feather mites

There are several types of these including *megninia columbae* and *liponyssus sylvarium*. As the name suggests they can be found around the quills and feathers, producing an obvious scale appearance. An appropriate dusting powder such as pyrethrum or similar, is best administered on a regular basis.

## g) Scaly leg mite (cnemidocoptes mutans)

They are particularly apparent on game birds including pheasant as well as Guinea Fowl. Usually when standards of hygiene are good, you should not be troubled by these mite. They usually show up as white, grey like scabs on the claws and legs of the affected birds. The mites are not just a skin surface problem, but can actually cause the birds to go lame.

There are treatments available over the counter, but consultation with a vet would be recommended. A 50:50 solution of paraffin mixed with lorexanne it quite an old remedy that seems to work. The legs are dipped in the solution 2 times per week until the problem has disappeared. Usually with a toothbrush, gently brush the affected parts.

Applying generous amounts of petroleum jelly can soften the scales to begin with.

It is then recommended that the affected legs are dipped into surgical spirit once per week, for up to 4 weeks. Again apply petroleum jelly afterwards.

Once again, if you are in any doubt please do not hesitate to consult with a veterinarian for their advice on treatments.

## h) Red mite (dermanyssus gallinae)

These are tiny, less than 1mm long and despite the name are grey in color. As they are nocturnal blood suckers, once they feed, they turn red. They generally live in crevices within the infrastructure of the building. They do not live on the bird like some parasites, but crawl from the cracks and crevices they inhabit to feed on the birds. Sign of an infestation can first be seen as the birds show signs of skin irritation and anemia. They can often be spotted on eggs that have not been collected until late in the day. You can usually see their droppings that appear as red spots on eggs.

There are products available that treat both housing and birds, such as Diatom or Smite powder. Lindane otherwise known as gamma benzene hexachloride was always considered to be a powerful insecticide, and is still used in some countries. This is usually what is known as a second line treatment, i.e. if other treatments have failed. However, because of environmental contamination and cancer risk etc, since 2006 this has been banned in over 50 countries and restricted in about 30 others.

Whichever remedy is used, treatment is needed for the whole house, which should be sprayed, and the birds regularly dusted with a powder such as pyrethrum.

### i) Mites: (acari)

These are prolific parasites that occur worldwide and affect most bird species.

They generally feed every 2 to 4 days for several hours but can be up to 11 hrs. They can usually be found on the neck and back of the bird. When not feeding on poultry, they will reside anywhere in the poultry house such as litter, paper, wood, plastic etc and usually in cracks and crevices.

Signs of a problem can include; thirst, low egg production, poultry that seem to avoid the areas most affected and lack of condition with dull looking feathers.

Recent research on the control of red mite conducted by UK and Danish researchers discovered a fungus that can kill red mite. The spores of the fungus effectively spread throughout the mite eventually killing it. The dead mite infected with the fungus creates more spores that spread and infect and kill more mites. There has also been recent research conducted to develop a vaccine as well as an antibody that reacts against the mite.

### j) Fleas: (siphonaptera)

Fleas can prove problematic to poultry although they are usually associated with affecting mammals such as domestic cats and dogs. They are not host specific and tend to seek different hosts on a regular basis. They are therefore not as problematic as other parasites.

Fleas can be found under the wings and around the breast and cloaca.

You can try smearing the affected parts with petroleum jelly or something similar.

## 6) GENERAL GUINEA FOWL DISEASES

Guinea Fowl are exceptionally hardy among domestic poultry. However they are susceptible to certain diseases and ailments. These usually relate to either respiratory, or parasites, which you have read about above.

Among poultry breeds Guinea Fowl do seem to have a better resistance to certain diseases. These include, lymphoid leukosis, Marek's disease and bronchitis.

The following is not exhaustive of all the possible diseases or ailments that can afflict Guinea Fowl, but the most common are covered. Again, please do not assume that the following are likely to affect your birds. They are noted here as diseases that at some time have been know to affect Guinea Fowl. Also please note, that the disease is described along with symptoms, but I have deliberately omitted treating these. A lot of the diseases can be quite serious and if you suspect your Guinea Fowl may be suffering any, I would always recommend seeking professional veterinary advice.

### a) Infectious enteritis.

This is a serious infection and is specific to Guinea Fowl. It can be devastating to whole flocks.

**Symptoms include**: trembling/ shivering, appetite loss, prostration, diarrhea which last approximately 1 week. There is a high death rate. A veterinarian should be consulted immediately.

## b) Ostitis

This is a condition that effectively causes the head and eyes to swell. It is possibly caused by a mycoplasmic infection or some sort of virus. It can affect a whole flock or just a single bird. The weight of the head causes the bird to droop the head.

## c) Coccidiosis (Canker) (Protozoa) (trichomonas gallinae)

This is one of the main diseases that affect the general poultry population on a worldwide basis. It is usually a disease occurring from March to October, or there about. Coccidia is a large group of parasites. There are said to be over 30 different strains of this disease. Outbreaks can cause serious problems for the Guinea Fowl flock. In this respect early diagnosis is necessary as soon as possible. The disease is spread from the feces of an infected bird and picked up by other birds feeding. It is a condition that seems to spread only by the birds picking up food that has been infected. On free range it can be spread initially from wild bird droppings, as well as the aforementioned infected feces and food.

Keets are particularly vulnerable, which is why it is important to administer medicated feed as a preventative measure.

**Symptoms:** The oesophagus and crop are largely affected and become ulcerated. A loss of appetite as well as a pungent odor from the bird are first signs. The birds have an extreme thirst and usually have a diarrhea that is whitish or sometimes brown in color. They can also appear lethargic, have general listlessness, seem uninterested and have problems with coordination.

The disease is generally spread by physical contact and this can be, via clothing, equipment and footwear. It can also be spread airborne between poultry houses in commercial establishments. Oocyst spores can easily grow and establish themselves on damp dirty litter, contaminated feeders and drinkers, insufficient ventilation and overcrowding.

Once again apart from obvious symptoms, lab testing confirms the disease. This is a serious disease if untreated and should again be diagnosed by a veterinarian.

**Treatment**

The reverse of the bad management noted above, such as cleanliness, hygiene control, correct ventilation, and disinfection etc. Litter may become damp because of leaking pipe work or drinkers not working correctly.

## d) Hexamitiasis and Trichomoniasis

Hexamitiasis and Trichomoniasis are **protozoan parasites and** are generally associated with damp conditions where the soil is stale or sour. They can be spread very easily from infected feces on the keepers boot.

Symptoms of this include an ill looking bird with yellowish diarrhea. Once again prevention is better and ensuring the ground isn't allowed to become sour and overly soiled should ensure breakouts are prevented.

Sour overused land can also be a major cause of worm infestations. A tell tale sign of this condition is when the birds appear hungry, but when picked up are light and thin.

### e) Pulmonary mycosis or mycotic pneumonia (aspergillosis)

This is caused by the fungus *aspergillosis fumigates*. Fungus or mold is spread on infected grain or shavings. It can also occur as a result of feeding grain that has gone moldy, or bedding that has gone damp and allowed to go moldy. Large commercial poultry buildings have also been known to report the infection from build ups of infected dirt in the heating and ventilation system.

**Symptoms:** the disease affects the lungs and can therefore cause labored breathing and if particularly serious the bird literally gasps for air. You should not confuse this with the Guinea Fowl tendency to pant when hot or thirsty, and therefore breath through their mouth. They will also be generally unwell, lacking energy and a lack of appetite. This can affect keets and death rates are up to and around 50%. It is often necessary to cull affected birds, when there is a large flock. Any infected bedding has to be removed and destroyed. Affected and infected areas must be disinfected. Once again professional advice from a vet should be sought.

### f) Fowl Pox

Can be transmitted by either insect bites or wild birds. Distinctive white/yellow scabs appear on exposed parts of the body. They can turn quite hard and dark. Inflamed eye lids can occur, but not always. Once again the birds generally lose appetite and appear unwell. Mouth and nasal passages can develop yellow patches that make breathing difficult. The birds should be isolated at the first sign of symptoms and professional help and diagnosis sought. The external

manifestations of the infected birds can be treated. Immunization of the rest of the flock is often successfully undertaken as a preventative measure.

### g) Mycoplasma and E Coli

There are a number of micro organisms such as mycoplasma synoviae, mycoplasma melegrides, and the E coli group that can infect the birds.

The following symptoms are general, and so they do not all occur with the specific organism : General malaise and lack of energy, bronchial and nasal cavities are affected and so coughs develop as well as watery eyes and nostrils.

Symptoms can also include anaemia, also abscesses in the legs causing lameness. Although treatment with antibiotics is possible, as with salmonella, serious cases are often culled.

As with many of these cases, prevention is a far better solution than cure. In that respect rigorous hygiene should be in place.

### h) Mycoplasma gallisepticum and Mycoplasma synoviae:

These diseases cause chronic respiratory and related diseases such as conjunctivitis in a number of poultry and game birds.

The spread of the disease is generally by respiratory means. This can be from infected feeders, drinkers, as well as vermin and wild birds. It is thought however that the diseases will die off outside of the host, within 24 hours.

Symptoms include: breathing difficulty, nasal discharge, sneezing and conjunctivitis. The joints can also be affected.

Professional testing is necessary to diagnose the condition

### Treatment

As usual strict hygiene, regular cleaning and disinfection as well as strict bio-security is necessary.

### i) Candidosis:

A number of habitation problems can cause this to develop. Generally poor hygiene along with high damp, humidity and overcrowding. Too much antibiotic dosage in the same way that this can kill good bacteria in humans. This becomes a problem when the good bacteria is not replaced. It has to be said however, that sometimes the birds will contract *candida*, in healthy, clean, uncrowded conditions.

**Symptoms include:** Keets in particular show loss of appetite, lack of energy, fit-like neck movements, loss of coordination. Any secretions will look greyish/white, and as the crop becomes affected it can feel quite solid. It is not one of the most serious diseases and although it is treatable, mortality in keets can affect 1 in 3

### j) Respiratory disease.

It is caused by a pneumonia organism. It is common amongst game birds and as such, Guinea Fowl. A nasal discharge is often seen and the face becomes swollen. Appetite loss is typical, as is weight loss. Antibiotics usually successfully clear the problem, but often the birds remain carriers of the disease.

The organism can develop quickly where draughts and poor ventilation are a problem. Mortality is common if unchecked.

### k) Bronchitis:

There exist a number of strains that have different symptoms, which include;

sneezing and sometimes kidney problems.

### l) Tuberculosis:

This is usually spread by feces from infected birds. It is contagious and it is sometimes necessary with serious outbreaks to cull the affected.

Symptoms include; weight loss that accompanies the birds lack of fitness, swelling joints and consequent lameness, growths can appear around the head, eyes and throat.

### m) Laryngotracheitis:

This is not a worldwide problem. However symptoms can be very serious and include, difficulty breathing. Mucous build up can be a serious problem, which can block the trachea sometimes causing death. Any that is coughed up by the bird, can be blood stained. There is an available vaccine as a preventative measure.

### n) Salmonellosis: (Salmonella)

There are hundreds of different types of the salmonella bacteria. Outbreaks usually require notification to the authorities.

However, only two seem to be a problem for Guinea Fowl.

Paratyphoid (*salmonella typhimurium*): Is contracted via infected food.

Symptoms include; lacking energy, greenish looking diarrhea, occasional vomiting, convulsions. Death will occur in a matter of days, however the birds can be treated if acted upon early enough

Pullorum or white diarrhea (*salmonella pullorum*). This can be transmitted by the infection in a number of ways such as infected equipment, or the boots and cloths of a keeper. Incubated eggs can be infected via an infected parent and consequently pass this onto the keet and then other keets in the brood. Infected birds usually huddle and appear ill and listless. As the name suggests, the diarrhea is usually white when keets are affected, and the unfortunate ones can die off quite quickly. Adult birds who can appear ill and produce diarrhea that is a greenish brown color, do not generally have as high a mortality rate as keets.

Once again professional diagnosis is needed and this is usually confirmed by a blood sample.

Treatment can be successful, but culling is sometimes necessary in serious cases. In the past it has been deemed that the culling of whole flocks is necessary.

## o) Salmonella Aspergillosis

This is usually caused by damp conditions as well a stale moldy food, that result in fungal spores developing. It is a respiratory condition and produces symptoms of obvious breathing difficulty such as outstretched necks. This can easily be avoided by ensuring the litter, floor covering is clean and dry and only the freshest food given. Any damp bedding needs to be replaced as soon as possible. You should also ensure that you spray the area with disinfectant on a regular basis.

In all cases if you have a bird or several that appear ill and not eating, and you are unsure of the problem, always isolate the birds and seek veterinary advice as soon as possible.

Salmonella is more often than not transmitted via mice, rats or wild birds. Hygienic conditions can make the situation worse as can stale, infected food.

## p) Fowl typhoid (salmonella gallinarum)

This was a major cause of poultry decimation in the past, however it is no longer a significant threat. North America, Europe and Australia have largely eliminated the problem. The disease in recent years has still had an effect on areas of South America, Africa and Asia. Many poultry including chickens, ducks pheasant, turkeys and of course Guinea Fowl are susceptible to the disease.

Bird hosts can carry the disease for a number of years and consequently pass this to the offspring. The disease can also be ingested through the mouth or respiratory intake.

There are a number of causes of the spread such as wild birds, insects, mammals and red mite.

**Symptoms**

Appetite loss, thirst, lack of energy, difficulty breathing, yellowish green diarrhea and generally looking unwell.

**Treatment**

Vaccines are often administered in at risk countries. Other than vaccination, the main control is high standards of cleanliness and hygiene. Birds that show signs should be removed and isolated from the flock to eliminate the possibility of spread.

## q) Pullorum: (salmonella pullorum)

The global incidence of (salmonella pullorum) is the same as Fowl typhoid (salmonella gallinarum). So not affecting North America etc, but potentially a problem in Asia, but said to affect some parts of Europe. In parts that are not affected this is said to be due to regular testing for the disease and culling of affected birds.

The spread is via an infected host during the reproduction process. Salmonella is thought to be able to survive on food and bedding/litter for up to 2 years or more. The disease can spread via a number of means such as contact with infected birds, as well as the birds picking up the disease whilst eating or drinking or generally scratching among the litter.

The frequency of the disease for newly infected hatches can be as high as 100%. Although generally the figure is around 50%. It is thought that up to 35% of these birds, can potentially become carriers.

Affected birds have a white diarrhea, and there is generally a smearing of this discharge around the feathers of the vent. The joints can also appear swollen.

### Diagnosis

A positive laboratory diagnosis is usually needed to confirm the presence of *salmonella pullorum*.

### Treatment

The disease is not thought to be easily treatable, although some medications can reduce the effects. Preventative control measures such as bio-security that reduce the chance of passing the disease from outside sources, is thought to be imperative. Regular testing will also keep a check of the health status of the birds and eliminate any potential carriers. In some cases, regardless of the size of the flock, culling is often seen as the most viable option. Culling means that you have to literally start from scratch with thoroughly cleansed and disinfected areas. Removal of any old bedding, food etc would also be necessary as is the re-stocking of birds positively tested to not carry any disease.

### r) Bird flu: (avian influenza)

This is a serious viral infection among poultry, that has in recent times become a major public health problem. There are 5 genre of the virus but only (*influenzavirus A*), is thought to be a problem to poultry. The disease can prove to be very damaging to bodily tissues and vital organs.

A number of outbreaks of this have occurred recently. Wild birds are said to be the main cause, due to migration from the Far East. However, modern day aircraft travel cannot be ruled out as a possible cause, as diseases can easily pass continents on a daily basis. As previously mentioned, regardless of the initial source, strict measures should be in place on all poultry farms and units, regardless of size. It is too easy for visitors to pass a disease from place to place.

Wild birds undertaking migration across continents are thought to be a major cause.

The spread can occur from sources outside of the flock and geographical location of the premises. In this respect, bio-security is vital to restrict the spread. It is possible for the virus to be spread by airborne means, and depending on the strain, can also survive for several weeks.

Symptoms include: indifference and lack of energy in the bird, lack of appetite, respiratory disease, a possible yellow/greenish diarrhea. Generally there is a high rate of mortality.

Although there have been a number of significant incidences of bird flu and subsequent cullings, there have only been a few incidences involving Guinea Fowl.

An accurate diagnosis of the virus would ideally be obtained from laboratory testing. However, testing kits are available that allow you to detect the presence of the virus from an infected sample.

### Treatment

Vaccines are said to be available that protect the bird against certain virus infections. However it is thought the virus most affecting poultry can infect the bird without the bird showing symptoms.

### s) Newcastle Disease: (avian paramyxovirus)

**Newcastle disease or Fowl Pest.** This is a virus that spreads via the feces of infected birds. It can generally affect poultry and game birds such as chickens, turkeys, pheasants etc. The Guinea Fowl, seem to be relatively immune to the disease. However, although they can exhibit no obvious symptoms, they can be carriers of the disease. In areas that this is a problem, immunization is advised.

This disease was first established in chickens in the early 20th century. The disease name comes from the place of the first known detection, in Newcastle Upon Tyne, England, UK.

Symptoms include: lack of energy, weight loss and diarrhea. In addition signs of nervous disorders can manifest such as paralysis of the limbs, lack of coordination, generally shaking of the muscles including the neck.

This is a contagious disease with a worldwide incidence.

Infected birds generally pass on the virus once the birds start to pass bodily excretions such as mucus and feces as well as airborne means. Infection to other birds therefore is via ingestion and also airborne. Ironically birds kept on a commercial basis in cages are far less susceptible than birds with direct contact to the floor litter. The virus can survive several years in a frozen state, but generally die off within several weeks without the host.

There are thought to be 3 forms of the virus and have various effects depending on which form the bird contracts. Again, symptoms can occur such as diarrhea that is generally colored green, as well as the aforementioned respiratory and neurological symptoms. Lack of egg production and soft shelled or shell-less eggs can also be a sign. Newcastle disease has also been associated as a secondary infection with other diseases such as *E-coli* and *Mycoplasma*.

Newcastle disease, unfortunately is not an easy disease to diagnose, even where accurate symptoms are established. Correct testing during post mortem is necessary to confirm a diagnosis.

### Treatment

Vaccination is the usual method of preventing an outbreak. As always cleanliness, hygiene, regular disinfection, strict management and bio-security are the most positive measures to prevent an incidence of the disease.

Newcastle disease is of major concern for chicken mortality but not so much Guinea Fowl, in parts of Africa and Asia.

### t) Thick leg disease: (osteopetrosis)

Effectively this is a bone disorder affecting the legs and wings. The disorder manifests itself as an actual thickening of the main leg and wing bones.

This can be passed on as a hereditary disease from hen to chick.

Obvious physical signs can confirm the disease to an extent, but laboratory testing would need to confirm this.

**Treatment**

There seems to be no vaccine that can prevent the disease. Quite often the only solution is to ensure that any birds obtained are free of the virus.

## u) Blackhead disease: (histomoniasis)

The disease was first discovered in the late 19th century. It affects domestic poultry including turkeys and game birds.

The caecal worm is said to initially transfer the disease to the birds via ingestion of the eggs of the caecal worm. The infected birds then act as hosts thus spreading the disease further. Free range soil contamination can take place as the eggs are said to exist up to a 3 year period. Earth worms are also said to sometimes act as a host, which obviously birds can ingest.

**Symptoms:**

Weight loss, depression and yellow feces are initial signs of a problem. Mortality is said to be high, with incidence happening within a week.

Again other than physical symptoms the surest diagnosis is by laboratory testing.

**Treatment**

The disease can be treated but prevention is seen as the most effective means of managing the disease.

## v) Avian diphtheria (infectious laryngotracheitis)

The disease has a global presence and is highly contagious. It is a respiratory disease that affects domestic poultry such as chickens and Guinea Fowl.

It is also known to affect peafowl and pheasant. The young birds are most at risk, however, it can affect any age group. Male birds are said to be more susceptible than female.

The virus can be inhaled or ingested via airborne means or fecal and mucous excretions. There are no reports that the virus is present in a newly hatched chick. The disease is largely present in the respiratory tract. Birds can be carriers of the disease and yet show no outward signs of illness or symptoms.

Birds can be found dead without prior warning of the disease. The disease can also manifest as a sudden acute attack of coughing. They can also show symptoms of conjunctivitis, sinus problems, eye swelling and closure as well as nasal discharge. There can also be mild forms of the above that do not necessarily result in death.

Again other than physical symptoms the surest diagnosis is by laboratory testing.

**Treatment**

Vaccination is usually the best control method as well as bio-security measures. Vaccinations in certain countries should be considered as a safeguard against diseases that are commonplace to that country.

## w) Ornithobacterium rhinotracheale.

This is quite a recent disease with incidences occurring worldwide. It can affect many types of poultry including chickens, duck, geese, turkey, pheasant and Guinea Fowl to name a few. It has not been known as a high public health risk, and the mortality rate of affected birds has been quite low; up to 7%. It also generally affects young birds up to

26 weeks old.

Once again, affected carriers can spread this via the reproduction phase. Therefore hatcheries can easily pass the disease through infected eggs.

**Symptoms**

Mild respiratory symptoms can initially occur such as sneezing and coughing. This can lead to more distressing symptoms and can lead in some cases to pneumonia. Autopsy usually reveals a white creamy discharge in the air cavities of the skull.

Is not always easy as the symptoms can mimic a number of other diseases such as E-coli.

**Treatment**

Vaccination is often seen as an effective means of dealing with the disease. However, as treatments such as antibiotics have shown bacterial resistance, then eradication is not 100% certain.

## x) Fowl Cholera (avian pasteurellosis)

This is caused by a bacteria which affects the alimentary and respiratory tracts. It can be spread a number of ways including, feces from infected birds, wild birds, rodents or mechanically brought in via equipment and vehicles

**Symptoms include:** thirst, labored breathing, diarrhea that is green/yellow in color, general listlessness, swollen joints with birds going lame or simply found dead. It is therefore another serious disease and again the death rate is high. Once again it is very important to contact a veterinarian as soon as you suspect this.

## y) Fowl cholera (pasteurellosis)

The presence of the disease has been known worldwide. It is a contagious disease with a high incidence of death among birds affected.

Carriers of the disease are quite wide spread. So many birds and mammals can transmit the disease. Most if not all poultry are at risk of contracting the disease.

Disease spread is known via a number of sources such as wild birds, rodents and domestic pets such as cats and dogs. Although transmission of the disease can occur between poultry flocks, infected eggs do not seem to be a cause of spread.

**Symptoms**

General symptoms found in a lot of diseases are common to fowl cholera. These include, mucous discharge, diarrhea, listlessness and weight loss.

Professional laboratory tests are required for a positive diagnosis.

**Treatment**

Antibiotics and other treatments are commonly used to combat the disease. As with similar cases, vaccination is seen as a preventative measure. Strict hygiene and bio-security is also necessary to prevent future outbreaks or spread.

# CHAPTER TWELVE

# BEHAVIORAL PROBLEMS

T his chapter will deal with common behavioral problems that you may encounter with your Guinea Fowl. You will also find some solutions and suggestions of how to deal with them.

## 1) AGGRESSION

### *Aggression towards new flock members*

Guinea Fowl can be quite aggressive and hostile to other Guinea Fowl and other poultry you may have. Although this can have serious consequences, their aggressive tendencies can at times prove to be very useful to the flock and other poultry. They have been known to attack predators such as rats, snakes, birds of prey etc.

However, aggressive behavior that results in bullying and pecking, is a sure sign that the birds are not happy. The so called 'pecking order' will manifest itself regardless, as the birds naturally wish to assert their authority, or let others know to keep out of their way. If the birds are not happy, then they will become stressed and therefore less productive.

Guinea Fowl can be very aggressive to any newcomers to the flock. This is one of the main reasons why it is never advised to bring in new birds to an existing flock. A lot of aggressive hen pecking can take place that can lead to injuries. You should take any attack seriously, as they can be merciless and in some cases a kill another bird. They can also show odd behavior to members of the flock that you maybe have to isolate, because of sickness or injury. When those birds are returned to the flock, sometimes one or two birds will pick on them as if they are strangers. It is hard to say what the reason for this is. Maybe they easily forget birds they only knew several days previous, or perhaps they are punishing them for seemingly deserting the flock in some way. A lot of animal species adopt a 'survival of the fittest' approach and so attack weak or sick animals, There is a strong likelihood that once the new member becomes more familiar, and the existing flock realize they are no threat, they should settle down.

## Coexisting with other poultry

So Guinea Fowl can be aggressive towards other Guinea Fowl, and poultry. Given adequate space however, they will coexist quite happily, with only occasional skirmishes. If they have the choice and opportunity, they will roam and forage, in some cases miles, from dawn till dusk. Some keepers do not have the luxury of free range and so have to contain the Guinea Fowl in a wired or netted enclosure.

You will see Guinea Fowl living happily with other poultry, but they do have a tendency to dominate the others, or at least attempt to dominate. They can be aggressive towards other poultry or weaker members of their own flock. Apart from the inevitable pecking order, they can become particularly aggressive during mating season.

Male Guinea Fowl will tend to fight each other as mating season approaches and in fact during mating season. This is common with many animal species as the strongest and fittest vie for female attention and mating rights. Injuries may or may not occur, depending on the resistance the birds put up. But fights can become violent and in some cases fatalities occur. Chases are often a common occurrence and this can be relentless.

## What if there is a serious attack?

However if you notice any kind of severe attack then you should remove the injured bird and keep it in one of your separate areas. Unfortunate as this is, once some birds draw blood then they will not stop until the victim is dead. Using a red light as a calming effect

Many keeper use a red light inside the hen house over night. Guinea Fowl are not particularly good at seeing in the dark. This will therefore allow them to see the surroundings and get down from the roost and back up again without risking injury. If the building you have is predator and vermin proof, they should be fine in the dark. If you suspect vermin such as rats are getting in, the Guinea Fowl may protest and certainly if they cannot see what is going on.

The light is dim enough that it does not seem to disturb them. White lights tend to be too bright for them and cause them to be agitated and possibly aggressive towards others. The red light seems to have a calming effect.

## Keeping them enclosed

Your Guinea Fowl may predominantly free range, and on occasion you have to keep them enclosed, perhaps because of bad weather or predator threat. In this case, do not be surprised if you notice your guineas marching back and forth pressing against the fencing, trying to get out. They will appear to be in a panic, and you will probably be anxious to let them out. Do not worry about seeing this as they will no doubt settle down after a few days, and get used to the fact that they cannot get out to free range.

## *Problems with free range foraging*

If your guineas are to free range, they do not need a lot of encouragement to start exploring and foraging. If you do have flower or vegetable beds, and the guineas start making a nuisance of themselves, destroying plants, you may need to net or fence these areas. If you find they go into these areas in search of insect pests and weeds, and do not appear to be destroying plants, then of course leave them to it.

## 2) PROBLEMS WITH NOISE

## *a) Why are Guinea Fowl noisy?*

There are a number of reasons Guinea Fowl at whatever age can be noisy. It is simply in their nature to alert their immediate flock of any impending danger. Obviously the by-product of this is that every one within ear shot knows this as well. Once you realize that this is in some cases a life saving measure to not only them, but other animals, you will no doubt fully sympathize.

Unfortunately the problem occurs when this becomes a nuisance to neighbors. In the African wilds then this is vital for their self preservation.

However, in our modern times and environments it can seem extreme and over the top.

As Guinea Fowl tend to be excitable they should be kept free from surprises such as anything that is likely to disturb them.

They are not always noisy, and are generally quiet until disturbed, but once they start, it can be a while before they stop. It is generally assumed that they call out when there is an intruder or predator lurking, but they can easily start shrieking in unison, if one of the other birds does something unusual, or simply flies over the enclosure.

You will also find that they will quieten when it is dark. This is one of the reasons you need to confine them over night as soon as light fades. However, early dawn light can cause Guinea Fowl to be noisy. With this in mind, you should make sure that little or no outside light can be seen from inside. You may have to put shutters up at the coop windows. But as soon as dawn breaks the Guineas will want to be out, and will start making a noise.

The common or helmeted Guinea Fowl is therefore not ideal for communities where neighbor relations may be a problem. However, this should by no means should deter anyone from considering Guinea Fowl as a pet in their own right, or an addition to other poultry they may have. Guinea Fowl are generally not seen as any worse than Geese, who can be quite vocal in a similar way.

With correct understanding of how Guinea Fowl behave and react, you can effectively manage them with very little problem.

Guinea Fowl are vocal and communicate with each other quite often. Anything that disturbs them will be reason enough for them to sound an alarm, until the danger passes, or they are sure they will come to no harm. They can become excitable during feeding, or if one finds a food source and calls the others. They are also known to become quite vocal at roosting time. They do not discriminate as to their noise level as the whole point is that is alerts the rest of the flock, who may be some distance away.

## b) Young keets and noise

There are a number of reasons and causes that you could encounter. The following hopefully sheds some light on some of the reasons and remedies you can take to alleviate the problem. First of all, younger keets as they grow can be more vocal than the adults. The main reason for this seems to be that everything is strange at first, and once they realize the new surrounding is not a threat they should quieten. They will still shriek and call out when anything unusual occurs to them, but this should disappear as the cause disappears, or they realize it isn't a threat. It is no different to a dog barking at a stranger.

This is why it is important to get the young keets as used to their surroundings as possible. It is also for this reason that any mature birds you introduce, will behave in much the same way as the young keet. Everything is strange and new, and it takes time to settle. But it is still considered that the safest solution to this potential problem is to refrain from purchasing adult birds and raise your own keets from day old or eggs you incubate.

## c) Noisy hens

Guinea Fowl hens are said to make more noise than the male cock birds. For this reason if the noise level is likely to be a problem, then you may be better keeping only male guineas. The male is only known to make a one syllable continuous sound. The female sound is a two syllable repetition, but she has the ability to mimic the male one syllable sound.

### d) Keeping male birds only

Ironically, many males on their own will cohabit reasonably well. Some experienced keepers will even advise keeping only male Guinea Fowl. This is usually if noise is a problem, because as noted, male Guineas are considered quieter than the female.

### e) Why a flock is noisy

What can also cause them to be more disturbed and vocal than normal is when the group is split up. So if one or two fly over the fence, or left out to roost in a tree over night, they will make a commotion calling to each other. It is as if they are calling and communicating with each other, to make sure they are all safe. It is also perhaps the main group telling the others to come back. You should therefore notice that as long as the group is together they will not be as noisy. Of course this does not mean they will not make a noise when something strange, or a predator appears.

## 3) WING CLIPPING

### a) About Wing Clipping

Wing clipping isn't a behavioral problem as such. However, it is included here as a remedy to the problem of Guinea Fowl that fly beyond the enclosure or your property.

The point of wing clipping is that in an enclosure or fenced off pen, the birds cannot fly over the fence. Some people are averse to wing clipping as it reduces the birds chance of escaping from a predator. Wing clipping should therefore only be done if the birds are to remain in the enclosure and not free range as well. Part of having the ability to fly is that this exercises and strengthens both the wing and chest muscles. It is certainly more humane than some of the procedures such as pinioning. Pinioning is a procedure carried out to keets within the first 7 days. The procedure involves cutting the tip of one wing up to the 'thumb' of the wing. This prevents flight feathers from growing and unlike feather clipping, is permanent.

It is thought that when keets are clipped at the earliest opportunity, and then the feathers are allowed to grow back, that this affects their effectiveness at flying well.

### b) Do Guinea Fowl fly often?

Guinea Fowl are not known as flying birds, but make no mistake, they are effective fliers when they need to.

This is generally in short bursts, if they are startled or need to escape danger. In the wild they will generally be found roosting in tall trees, so it is no surprise that you may find them fly up to a tree or even the roof of your house.

### c) How to Clip the Wings

If you have a fence that is high enough, you may find that clipping the feathers prevents them from flying high enough over the fence. You can find many excellent videos on Youtube giving instruction as to how best to clip the wings. Basically what this involves is holding your birds. Fanning/opening the full wing. You will notice the first 10 or so feathers are larger than the others, and look as if they are in two parts. The first main feathers are known as the primary feathers, and these are the ones you cut. The other feathers are the secondary feathers and you do not cut these. You can probably hold the bird under your arm and do it yourself. But it is best to get someone to help you, as they can start to struggle and you can easily panic them.

Also, please only cut the feathers off one wing, as this unbalances them if they try and fly. If you clip both wings then they will still be able to fly to an extent. Some suggest that the left wing is the best side, but others will tell you it doesn't make that much difference. You ideally need to watch one of the Youtube videos for proper instruction. You are unlikely to find a specific video for Guinea Fowl, as most are for chickens. However the principal is the same for both.

Be careful not to draw blood when clipping

You need to take enough off each feather for it to be effective, but you do need to be careful not to cut too far towards the wing. The feathers contain a blood supply and you certainly do not want to cut into that and draw blood. If you do happen to draw blood you can use flour on the affected area, which should stem the bleeding. Or you can take a hand towel and squeeze this reasonably tightly over the affected area.

### d) What if you do not want to clip the wings?

If you permit your Guinea Fowl to free range, they may decide to wander beyond your property. If you are against the idea of wing clipping, you may have to start discouraging them from wandering too far. This may require letting them know they shouldn't wander beyond your boundary, by herding them away from these areas. There is no guarantee that doing this will work, but if you do it enough times, they may soon get the message. This is particularly important near open roads. Some Guinea Fowl have no fear of roads and can often be seen marching down a road and paying no heed to traffic. You could soon have road kill on your hands if you are not careful.

### e) Open top pens

If you intend to have open top pens, and you allow juvenile keets out, you will probably have to clip their wings. As you know, with adult birds you clip the primary feathers to approximately half their size. In adult birds and maybe more so with juvenile keets, you should check this every month or so. Depending on the age of the bird, the feathers can grow back quite quickly. You do not want to neglect this and find that your birds are flying over, never to be seen again. When clipping juvenile keets, be very careful not to cut into any quills with an obvious blood source.

# CHAPTER THIRTEEN

# GENERAL GUINEA FOWL INFORMATION

The following topics are intended to fit in with everything we have covered so far. However, because they are relatively short topics, they are included here as general information. You will find extra information in this short chapter covering training, cleaning, molting, dust bathing etc. Please note, the topics are listed in no particular order of importance.

## a) How do Guinea Fowl deal with cold weather?

traumatize them. They will of course need exercise and you should not take a fall of snow as a sign that you should

As previously mentioned, despite their relatively warmer origins of Africa, Helmeted Guinea Fowl, cope surprisingly well with extreme winter temperatures. Again, we have already mentioned that this is not the case with Vulturine or Crested Guinea Fowl. The following offers an insight into how Guinea Fowl who have not seen snow before are likely to react.

The first sighting of snow will be strange to the Guineas at first, but eventually their natural curiosity will no doubt get the better of them and they will begin to explore. If you have any that seem reluctant to venture out of the coop, then you can either leave them, or try and coax them out somehow. But you do not want to force them out and

keep them locked up. They do not like been confined for too long and this only promotes restlessness and hostility towards each other.

## b) Guinea Fowl as a meat product

It is not the intention of this book to go into any great detail about Guinea Fowl as a meat product. However, the following is a very brief introduction into the subject.

As you know, the common Guinea Fowl have become a popular addition for poultry enthusiasts and hobbyists. They have also been known as a useful food source for centuries. In recent times Guinea Fowl have been mass produced for an ever growing consumer market.

There is no getting away from the fact that Guinea Fowl meat is popular and in demand. From ancient times in Egypt, Greece and Rome and later in Europe and the USA, Guinea Fowl have been reared as a food product.

As the demand for free range foods have increased so has a demand for Guinea Fowl meat. For example in 2008, Waitrose in the UK, reported an increase in their sale of Guinea Fowl meat of 41%. There is no denying the fact that as a meat product, Guinea Fowl is highly nutritious. It is high in protein, no real fat content and rich in vitamins and minerals.

Guinea Fowl are now said to be mainly produced in Europe, although a considerable percentage is produced in the U.S.A. Within Europe the main producers and exporters of Guinea Fowl meat are France, Belgium and Italy. In 2008 it was recorded that around 38 million birds were reared, and of these birds ¾ were said to in France.

## c) MOULTING

The birds will moult, that is, shed old feathers for new growth, a couple of times per year. This is usually after the breeding season from late October. Again, you will notice that this will be at a time when the Guinea hens have stopped laying eggs. The reason for this not taking place during breeding season is that the birds natural bodily resources are limited during this time. They need to utilize available protein and other nutrients towards reproduction. When the birds moult, this puts extra stain on the birds resources as the new feathers need available food sources to replicate. They also tend to moult to a partial extent during winter. You should be careful to monitor the temperature inside the building, because until the birds are fully feathered again they will be vulnerable to serious temperature drops.

## d) IDENTIFICATION BANDS

This is a random piece of information that many keepers have found very useful, particularly as Guinea Fowl tend to look the same. Obviously if you have birds of different colors, then identification should be easy. However, a good useful idea to identify your birds perhaps for breeding purposes, is to use colored leg bands or other such identification tags. You can usually purchase these from most poultry suppliers.

## e) IDENTIFYING THE SEX OF GUINEA FOWL

To the untrained eye, sexing of the Guinea Fowl is not easy. A professional with the correct equipment can sex a keet at a relatively young age. The cloaca, which is the only orifice that Guinea Fowl and other birds have. Unlike humans and other animals who have two rear orifice, one that is purely for the expulsion of feces and the other for reproduction and urinating. Birds on the other hand have the one opening known as the cloaca, which combines both defecating and reproduction. It is possible to open the cloaca and view inside. The trained person can manipulate the opening and view whether the bird has a penis, which is seen as a fleshy appendage.

The pelvic cavity of the female should also be wider, to allow eggs to pass through. In more mature birds this can be roughly gauged by a 2 or 3 finger width.

Professionals in large hatcheries use specialist equipment and procedures to sex day old keets. But these procedures and successful diagnosis are probably beyond even the most experienced keepers. The experienced keeper would be able to sex the birds as they reach maturity up to 6 months of age.

The other way of telling the difference is the size of the wattles. The male wattles are noticeably larger and thicker than the female. So if you have a number of them together, you should be able to tell the difference.

Another sign of a male Guinea Fowl is that they will stand upright a lot more than the female, who will spend a lot of time picking about on the ground. Males also tend to appear leaner than a female.

## F) DUST BATHING

Guinea Fowl will want to take regular dust baths so you should ensure that you can prepare at least one area for them. If they are free range, they will no doubt find dusting areas for themselves.

As Guinea Fowl bathe by dusting and not water, they need access to an area that has a mixture of dry fine soil, perhaps mixed with sand. It is also best if they can dust in a warm, sunny area. Any designated dusting areas should be treated with some sort of dusting/lice powder. This will help the birds deal with any lice and parasites. The whole point of the birds dusting is that as they lay in the dust and spread dust into their feathers, this helps dislodged parasites such as lice that attach themselves to the plumage of the bird.

The action of dusting combines the dry abrasive soil/sand, which both cleanses the skin and removes parasites attached to the feathers. These are finally dispelled when the bird shakes the feathers out and begins preening.

## Dust bath

You can easily make shallow dusting boxes, which should be made approximately twice the size of the bird to allow it to move about. If you have space for a whole pit then try to accommodate several at the same time. You can easily make these out of planks of wood approximately 4 to 6 inches (10.2 cm to 15.2 cm) deep. The base of the box can be ½ inch (1.3 cm approx) plywood or similar. The wood can be easily screwed together. The contents should be a dry mixture of whatever soil is natural to the area you are. If this is soil, ash, peat etc or some combination, it is often a good idea to mix in sand as well. In fact sand as a substitute is excellent as a dust bath for birds anyway.

## Communal dusting pit

As with many other activities associated with Guinea Fowl, they like to do things as a group. You will quite often therefore see them taking a dust bath together. This as I am sure you can image could cause a lot of mess. Again you could build your own pit to accommodate 4 to 6 birds, or whatever space you have.

Unlike roosting, where they will generally seek the same roosting spot, the same cannot be said for where they take a dust bath. So next time they may choose a different spot to create a new dust bath or potential mess for a flower bed. It is not always easy to catch them in the act of creating a dust bath as this will take them 5 or 10 minutes to scratch a hollow. Other than maybe destroying flower beds, some keepers do not mind this as they simply go along and fill the holes in.

## G) MUCKING OUT, CLEANING AND DISINFECTING.

As we have already found, a lot of diseases can be avoided by regular routine cleaning and disinfecting. Hopefully the chapter on health will have highlighted how serious some diseases can be. In addition, how important it is to regularly cleanse and disinfect any housing.

### Large scale management

A large scale producer would have all manner of controls in place to ensure this is routinely carried out. The poultry houses will be adequately stocked, with correct lighting, heating, ventilation, food and water. There are likely to be isolation areas that ensure when a building is entered, a change of boots and overalls, as well as washing the hands etc. Even when visitors arrive, they will be expected to disinfect their boots when they arrive and again when they leave. These are just basics of the controls that are likely to take place. Viruses and bacteria can and will exist within the housing infrastructure unless regular control with a suitable disinfectant is administered.

### Health and safety precautions on a small scale

Even as a hobby keeper of a few poultry or in this case Guinea Fowl, you are well advised to follow these sorts of measures yourself. There are far too many cases of whole flocks having to be destroyed because some disease such as salmonella or bird flu has infected the whole flock. These cases may not, but could be as a result of poor management and therefore hygiene measures that are lacking.

### Cleaning the hen house/coop

An accumulation of feces over time is likely to encourage disease growth and parasites. As a routine it is advisable to clean out the housing at least once per week. Of course if you operate a deep litter system, then the objective here is to top up the bedding with fresh shavings etc. By doing this the bedding stays dry and relatively fresh. This can then be cleaned out as often as you feel the need, sometimes up to 6 months later, depending on the condition and circumstances of your set up.

### Cleaning the hen house (Mucking out)

Remember that any droppings that you remove when 'mucking out', can be piled up for compost and later manure spreading on your garden or free range land. How often you clean the hen house is your choice. Again, some keepers like to do this once per week and leave a thin spreading of sawdust or shavings about 1" (2.5cm) thick. Others prefer to keep adding shavings/bedding and provide what is known as a deep litter. This is then cleared between one month and in some cases, once per year, depending on how thick you bed the area.

### How often should you clean (muck out) the enclosure?

It is not necessary in general that you are that meticulous that everywhere is sterile. But keeping on top of manure clearing and occasionally disinfecting areas, should keep things under control. If you are not keeping to a routine weekly or monthly cleaning and disinfecting, then you should gauge when you think it is time to do this. As long as bedding is dry and the birds are not walking about in fresh feces, then your birds should remain relatively disease free.

### Dirt from the outside run

The area where the birds run free may get particularly muddy, through weather conditions, overuse or bad drainage. If that occurs then consider either putting down gravel or make a solid concrete base near the entrance. The purpose of this is that as the birds come into the hen house, in theory at least, most if not all of the mud will be scraped off their feet. The gravel or concrete can be periodically washed down to avoid a build up of mud on those areas.

What if the outside area becomes sour or diseased?

If you have a relatively small outside grassy or soil area that you suspect is sour or potentially diseased, you can always borrow a friends cultivator, or hire one. This will turn over the soil between 6" and 9" (15.2 cm and 22.9 cm) deep. This will not only work any compacted manure into fresh soil, but expose worms and such like that the birds will love to pick through. This is also a good alternative to anyone who does not have the space for an extra run that will aid rotation and therefore regrowth.

### Disinfecting

Always disinfect areas on a regular basis and in particular disinfect incubators and brooding areas before and after use.

You should be vigilant where health and hygiene are concerned. Following a few simple guidelines on regular cleaning and disinfecting, will pay off greatly. You do not want to be faced with a disease or parasite infestation and then have all the associated problems that follow. It can be far more costly in terms of time and money.

### General health management

So ensure that the birds never have dirty or damp bedding for long. Powder birds, bedding and dust baths on a regular basis, with a suitable powder to prevent lice, mites and other parasites. Do not feed stale or moldy feed. Always use a pair of boots, whether rubber or otherwise, that always remain on your premises. The last thing you want is to visit another farm or poultry keeper in those boots and then bring any infection or disease back to your birds. In the same vein, if you have visitors, ensure you have a disinfection foot bath for them to dip their boots. Or better still, have them change into a spare pair of your rubber boots before they enter your poultry area.

At the very least wash your boots before entering and as you leave the area.

## 2) TRAINING YOUR GUINEA FOWL

### A) WHEN SHOULD YOU START TRAINING?

You ideally need to start training the keets as soon as possible. There is no need to worry while they are in the brooder but once they are in the main hen house, get them used to taking millet. Millet will be your best friend when you need your Guinea Fowl to come back to you or back to the coop.

## b) The secret weapon: White millet

Fowl.

When training your Guinea Fowl,

The key ingredient to be able to do this successfully is to use white millet. Many keepers will tell you of the benefits of using this treat. However, it has to be said from the start that white millet should only ever be given as a treat. Guinea Fowl love white millet, so once they discover this and realize they can get it from you, they will respond to your training. It will not have the same effect if you are giving them this all the time. Also whenever you call them like this, you should reward them with the treat.

### *Problems with feeding millet*

Incidentally, do not feed the millet in one spot if some of the birds start being aggressive to others and not allowing them to feed. If this is the case then you should scatter this wider, or give the dominant ones a feed first and then walk away and drop feed for the other birds.

## c) How to train Guinea Fowl

In the same way that you can train a dog to do all manner of tricks and commands by way of repetition and a reward, you will do the same with your Guinea

you are doing a couple of things. In the first instance you need them to recognize that the coop and the enclosure is their home and that it safe. This is the reason keepers will keep the keets restricted to the coop initially and then restricted to the coop and the run. This is important if your birds will eventually roam free range. When you initially confine them to the hen house you are effectively training them and saying that this is where you come for food, water and to roost. When you let them out into the run, it is like saying this is free range but you still have to return to the coop on a night. Once this has been done for several weeks or months when and if you do let the birds out, they will hopefully not need much encouragement to return to the enclosure. You certainly do not want them to get into the habit of roosting in trees. They are likely to be able to withstand any extreme temperatures as adults, but many Guinea Fowl are picked off by predators such as owls.

## First training steps

What you will be doing is sprinkling this on the ground for them to have a look at. Do not expect them to immediately peck furiously at this, but once they get a taste for it, this is probably how they will react. It is equally important to start using a call to them as you sprinkle it. It is up to you what call you make, but it needs to something like, "come on then' or 'Guinea millet' or even 'Guinea Fowl'. It is up to you what call sign you use, but please try and use the exact same phrase each time. You can also whistle or use a rattle or something at the same time.

## How long will this take?

So you will be looking at a time frame to free range your flock of between 6 and 10 weeks. Again, there is no race to see the birds leave the enclosed pen. The longer you leave it and ensure that on a daily basis they are getting the treat and coming back to you, then all the better. You can then rest assured that you have trained them all you can before letting them out of the pen/yard and out to free range.

## Why you should keep the keets locked up for the first 6 weeks

Whether or not you have no other poultry and your intended Guinea Fowl will be your first, the keets should remain indoors for at least 6 weeks. This is a vital training period that will get the keets accustomed to the home that feeds, waters and allows them a place to roost in safety. Once they venture outside you should have no problems with them returning, to roost.

This is why it is important to properly train the birds as young as possible. They should never be encouraged to roost outside in the surrounding trees. The Guinea Fowl from keets should be encouraged as much as possible to roost inside the hen house.

D) TESTING THE TRAINING

Once you let them out you can test your training to make sure they have understood. Pick a time when you have them all outside. Stand in the coop and with your millet to hand and call them in. They should flock back to the coop in search of their treat. Obviously you need to sprinkle this on the floor.

You should have had all of your flock come back into the shed. In the unlikely event that this is not the case, then you will need to continue the training for a bit longer.

I would certainly not attempt to let the birds out of the pen and free to roam until I was certain they would come back on command.

## Calling the your flock back

The second thing you have to be able to do with your flock of Guinea Fowl is to call them back to the enclosure when they eventually free range. This can help you in a number of ways. On a night time you need them back in to the coop to lock them up safely and for them to roost. It will be a lot quicker to call the birds back than to go and find them and try and herd them back.

## Herding Guinea Fowl

If you are ever in a position where you have to get the Guinea flock in by herding, then be very patient with this. They will generally stay together in their flock and so all you should ideally need to do is get to the back of them and gradually walk them in. You will of course have already left the run enclosure door propped open. You can then raise your arms out to the side and watch that they are moving towards the door and if you veer to one side move to that side. Some people prefer to use sticks for this as arm extensions.

The important thing is not to startle them with any sudden movements, and avoid using helpers that the Guinea Fowl do not know. Anything or anyone strange will only make them more nervous and flighty.

You may sometimes find that the flock splits up to the extent that you get most into the enclosure but some have veered off somehow. In this case try and get the ones that are inside the run to go into the hen house and shut the door. You can then leave the gate to the run open and attempt to round the others up.

### *What if one of your birds goes missing?*

There is not a great deal you can do if you find a missing Guinea. Your Guineas should now be adequately trained to know when to come home to roost. You may check everything late at night as a matter of routine and of course a bird that came home late needs to be coaxed back in. What you do not want is to leave the Guinea out all night and risk a predator attack. You may also sometimes find that a Guinea goes missing because she has gone broody on a nest somewhere. Unfortunately predators may on occasion kill one of your birds. If one of your birds has been missing for a day or longer, it may be best to just assume they have unfortunately been taken by a predator.

# CHAPTER FOURTEEN

# WEBSITES, RESOURCES & CONCLUSION

The following is intended as an introduction to a number of websites where you can buy essential supplies for your Guinea Fowl. These include coops, accessories and food in both the U.S. and U.K.

## 1) COOPS, EQUIPMENT AND FOOD SUPPLIERS

Please note: The following are a few suggestions for on-line poultry suppliers in both the USA and the UK. It is intended to give you a good start, locating various supplies that you will no doubt need. It is not intended as a definitive list, nor is the author in anyway recommending or endorsing any of these. They are considered to be good suppliers, but again it is up to you to do your own research and decide who you wish to deal with.

I would also suggest doing a Google search for additional suppliers. You will also no doubt have local suppliers in your area. Also please be aware that general pet stores usually have poultry items and feed, so please do check those also. Once you gain experience, you will no doubt have your own favorites. Once again, please also consider ebay as a likely supplier of products to purchase. I would always urge you to shop around, and not necessarily go for the cheapest, particularly where feed is concerned.

Please also note that at the time of press, the following web links were working. However, from time to time, pages get changed, deleted or a supplier goes out of business. If you find these do not work, please go to the route .com or .co.uk web address. Again, the author takes no responsibility for the availability of any of these, when you the reader comes to access them.

The following suppliers are categorized as either Hen Houses/Coops, General Poultry Supplies or Poultry Feed. You will find that some offer all three, so please browse the whole website.

## A) HEN HOUSE/COOPS U.S.

**Backyardchickens.com:**
Excellent resource center for DIY coops, accessories and general information.

*http://www.backyardchickens.com/atype/2/Coops*

**Horizon Structures:**
Provide a customized chicken houses/coops service

*http://www.horizonstructures.com/chicken-coops.asp*

**DIY Chicken Coops:**
They sell DIY plans as well as organic feed and other resources

*http://diychickencoops.com/*

**Hayneedle.com:**
sell ready-made coops, runs and kits, as well as plans.

*http://www.hayneedle.com/pets/chickencoops_185611?source=googleaw&kwid=chicken%20coops&tid=exact*

**Henspa Chicken Coops:**
Coops, accessories and other information.

*http://www.henspa.com/*

**EZ Clean Coops:**
Provide ready-made chicken coops or kits assemble yourself

*http://www.ezcleancoops.com/*

## My Pet Chicken:

They sell coops as well as plans for DIY. They also sell other supplies.

*http://www.mypetchicken. com/catalog/Chicken-Coops-c3. aspx*

*The following are a few additional websites that you may find useful.*

*http://guineas.com/links/ index.php#housing*

*http://guineas.com/fo- rum/*
*http://starstructuresmc. com/*

## B) HEN HOUSE/COOPS U.K.

## Chicken Coops Direct

*http://www.chickencoopsdi- rect.com/ppclp-chickencoops.ht m?t202id=9182&t202kw=chic kencoops uk&gclid=Cj0KEQiA mCyBRDx65nBhcmVtbIBEiQ A7zm8lWi8aiFA3Dxh6NsSWJ h1lsvL_VnQDcB6abLbNuG- MaoaAkZO8P8HAQ*

## Chicken Coops UK

*http://www.chickencoopsuk. net/*

## Flytes So Fancy

*http://www.flytesofancy. co.uk/chickenhouses/Chicken_ Coops.html*

## Cages World

*http://www.cagesworld. co.uk/c/Chicken_Coops.htm*

## Egg Shell Online

*http://www.eggshellonline. co.uk/chicken-coops-and-hous- es-for-sale-uk.html*

## Smiths Sectional Buildings

*http://www.smithssection- albuildings.co.uk/*

## Hen House World

*http://www.henhouse- world.co.uk/*

## The Chicken House Company

*http://www.thechicken- housecompany.co.uk/*

## Green Valley Poultry Supplies

*http://www.chicken-house. co.uk/*

## C) POULTRY EQUIPMENT/ SUPPLIES U.S.

## Farmtek:

Equipment and supplies for poultry

*http://www.farmtek.com/ farm/supplies/cat1a;ft_poul- try_equipment.html*

## Stromberg's Chicks & Game- birds Unlimited:

Equipment and supplies for poultry

http://www.strombergschickens.com/

**Tractor Supply Company:**
Equipment and supplies for poultry.

http://www.tractorsupply.com/en/store/search/chicken-equipment

**Fleming Outdoors:**
Equipment and supplies for poultry

http://www.flemingoutdoors.com/poultryfeeders.html

**Kemps Koops**

http://www.poultrysupply.com/products.php

**My Pet Chicken**

http://www.mypetchicken.com/catalog/Chicken-Supplies-c6.aspx?all=all

**Indiv**

http://www.indiv-eis.com/

**Cackle Hatchery**

http://www.cacklehatchery.com/page11.html

D) POULTRY EQUIPMENT/ SUPPLIES U.K.

**UK Poultry Supplies**

http://www.ukpoultrysupplies.co.uk/

**SPR Centre**

http://www.sprcentre.com/

**Moorlands Poultry**

http://www.moorlandspoultry.co.uk/

**Pet Supermarket**

http://www.pet-supermarket.co.uk/Category/Caged_Bird_Supplies-Chicken_Poultry

**Durham Hens**

http://www.durham-hens-poultry-supplies.co.uk/

**Farmer Bertie Poultry Supplies**

http://www.poultrysuppliesuk.co.uk/

**Hens For Pets**

https://www.hensforpets.co.uk/

**Ascott Dairy**

http://www.ascott-dairy.co.uk/poultry/

## E) POULTRY FEED U.S

**Blue Seal:**

*http://blueseal.com/products/poultry/home-fresh*

**Tractor Supply:**

*http://www.tractorsupply.com/tsc/catalog/chicken/chickenfeedtreats#facet:&productBeginIndex:20&orderBy:&pageView:grid&minPrice:&maxPrice:&pageSize:20&*

**Nutrena®**

*http://www.nutrenaworld.com/products/poultry/*

**Purina Mills:**
Sell all types of feed including for game birds

*http://purinamills.com/chicken-feed/*

*The following are additional websites that you may find useful*

*http://www.starmilling.com/poultry-index.php*

*https://www.hiprofeeds.com/products/usa/poultry*

*http://www.albersfeed.com/poultry*

*http://www.lionsgrip.com/producers.*

*html*
*http://www.heygatesfeeds.co.uk/general/poultry-feeds/*

*http://www.fancyfeedcompany.co.uk/products/layers_pellets.htm*

## F) POULTRY FEED U.K

**Small Holder Feed**

*http://www.smallholderfeed.co.uk/Products/Layers/Default.aspx*

**Green Valley Poultry Supplies**

*http://www.chicken-house.co.uk/acatalog/7.5_and_20_kg_bags_of_feed.html*

**Heygates**

*http://www.heygatesfeeds.co.uk/general/poultry-feeds/*

**Omlet**

*https://www.omlet.co.uk/shop/chicken_keeping/feed_and_treats/*

**Hi Peak**

*https://www.hipeak.co.uk/product-category/bagged-feeds/organic-layers-feed/*

**Organic feed**

*http://www.organicfeed.co.uk/Products/*

## Pet Supermarket

*http://www.pet-super-market.co.uk/Category/Caged_Bird_Supplies-Chicken_Poultry?f14=Food*

## UK Poultry Supplies

*http://www.ukpoultrysup-plies.co.uk/products/chicken-feed.html*

## Fancy Feed Company
*http://www.fancyfeedcom-pany.co.uk/products.htm*

## CONCLUSION

Hopefully you have read this far and have found the contents useful, informative and inspiring. There is a lot to consider when deciding to become any kind of poultry keeper. So whether you are a beginner or existing poultry keeper, hopefully the book has clarified what it is like to specifically keep Guinea Fowl. Again, there is a lot to consider and appreciate, and hopefully this book reflects that.

The intention of the book was not to overwhelm you the reader and put you off committing to a few Guinea Fowl, or maybe even a flock. The intention was simply to give you as broad an appreciation as possible, so that you are fully prepared and equipped to properly look after and appreciate these fascinating birds.

As you will realize, having read the various chapters, caring for Guinea Fowl does not necessarily come without its problems. However, with correct awareness and any kind of training you may wish to implement, many potential problems can be avoided. The health and welfare of the birds should go without saying, so please do everything you can to provide healthy food and a safe, protective environment. In essence, it doesn't take a lot to keep them happy and healthy. At the very least you should be providing the following: (i) A safe habitat that can be as simple or elaborate as you wish, providing it is predator and weather proof. (ii) Healthy, nutritious food and fresh water, daily. (iii) Regular health measures. Remember that regular mucking out and disinfecting can make all the difference towards healthy, disease free birds.

You do not need to follow everything contained within. It really is very simple to keep Guinea Fowl. They do not need much in terms of housing, but as much outdoor space as possible, is highly recommended. The chapters on breeding and incubating may or may not appeal to you, so if not, feel free to skip those chapters. Just make sure you feed them well and keep them safe and disease free.

Thank you for reading and I wish you much luck with your new adventure.

# INDEX

Made in the USA
Monee, IL
23 July 2023

39755907R00115